# ON EARTH AS IT IS IN SPAIN

- tracking the Spanish interior with the patron saint of
Spanish poets, St John of the Cross, 1542-91

*James Irvine*

## James Irvine

*with best wishes
to Marina.*

Published by James Irvine

Copyright © 2011 by James Irvine

ISBN 978-0-9570903-0-9

# ON EARTH AS IT IS IN SPAIN

# INSIDE SPAIN WITH ST JOHN OF THE CROSS – AN INTRODUCTION

Very small, very brave, this man Juan was a most attractive rebel. His whole life was a rebellion, not by confrontation but by alternative example. He was a rebel against absence of love.

Juan lived his life as a mystic, one of the great mystics of Christendom. But his mysticism was a path open to all, unhabituated by church custom. It is an opening as relevant to all people now as it was then.

And Juan was also a supreme lyric poet. His poems are among the most exquisite in the Spanish language. They speak to us of the highest experience of love.

To Spain, he is history, a footnote to a golden age. Born in extreme poverty in 1542. At the age of 21 a friar in the Carmelite Order. At the age of 35 kidnapped, held in solitary confinement and abused, for providing people with an example of humility and virtue that had become an embarrassment to the great and good of his Order. Escaped, rehabilitated and, at 46 years old, raised to a position of influence within the Order. Meanwhile, several times referred to the Inquisition on suspicion of heresy. Three years later removed from high office, reduced to the ranks and served with an edict of banishment from Spain. But within months, before being able to leave, he had died at the age of 49.

Those who knew him spoke of him in life as a saint, 'small in stature, great in the eyes of God'. Within 25 years of his death the collecting of affidavits for his beatification was underway. In 1675 Pope Clement X declared him beatified, blessed. In 1726 Pope Benedict XIII canonised him, a saint. He had become San Juan de la Cruz, St John of the Cross. In 1926 Pope Pius X declared him a 'doctor of the universal church'. And in 1952 he was recognised as patron saint of Spanish poets.

These were successive flashes of posthumous publicity for a man who, while living, had chosen the way of darkness. His was a life in which what was hid from sight, what was to be found only in darkness, was what was paramount. Through his writings, too, ran this refrain: lost to view, out of sight, unseen, hidden, secret, mystery, hiding place, darkened vision, blind, oblivion. He always set course for obscurity.

Along the paths of Spain I have followed Juan, seeking there what is hidden of the man, of his works and of his world. He travelled those paths in the course of duty again and again, north to south, east to west, back and forth, thousands of kilometres, sometimes by mule, mainly on foot. So, mainly on foot, I have travelled them too.

'In order to arrive at what you do not know, you must go by a way that you do not know', Juan wrote. If you want to know, go and see, I say.

# 1 ON THE MESETA

In Castile, one feels close to the past.  Closer to the past than to the present, sometimes.

I walk along a cart-track.  It lies in a shallow, green fold of land that hides me from the endless scorched-earth, all around, the high kingdom of Castile.  I pass a drift that leads the eye to barns and buildings, empty farmyards and apparently defunct vehicles.  Is this small settlement abandoned?  The great, baroque, red-brick church that dominates it certainly looks grassed in and moribund.

Cuckoos call.  Larks and hoopoes fly, and an occasional buzzard and a kite.

On either side of the track, waist-high barbed wire holds back undergrowth.

The path is gritty and I walk it in open sandals, with a pack on my back and a good staff, iron-tipped, in my right hand.  I walk at the old pace of one Castilian league each hour.  A useful distance, 5.6 kilometres, for measuring out the journey and the day.  One can make out one's next marker at about a league and reach it in about an hour.  I am to walk just three leagues, three hours, this morning, under a midsummer sky.

At a bend in the track, I am unhappy to see two beasts ahead.  Their great bulk is the colour of ochre.  They stand in my path nearly two hundred yards away, quite still.  They are cattle, as big as I have ever met, and I am afraid already.  I hope that they are not bulls but cows.

At one hundred yards it becomes clear that they are bulls.  Staff in hand, tapping regularly, I approach along the strait and narrow.  They simply stand and stare.  These are not spring-heeled toros bravos bred for the bullring.  These are like the massive stone toros de Guisando.

Since pre-history, the toros de Guisando have stood in a valley some 80 kilometres to the south of the path where my two attendant bulls now stand. Their valley is in the crumpled fault-line that pushes up between Ávila and Toledo and separates the two great plains that are the heart of Spain, Old Castile to the north and New Castile to the south.  People say

3

that the toros de Guisando were boundary markers between different celtiberian tribes. People say that Julius Caesar won a great victory nearby. But these are bulls and this is Spain, so Lorca says:

| | |
|---|---|
| ... y los toros de Guisando, | ... and the bulls of Guisando, |
| casi muerte y casi piedra, | all but death and all but stone, |
| mugieron como dos siglos | bellowed like two centuries |
| hartos de pisar la tierra. | weary of treading the earth. |
| No. | No. |
| Que no quiero verla! | How I do not wish to see it! |

How I do not wish to see my two bulls, so still in the path before me, all but death and all but stone. Only their heads, on a level with mine, swing to follow me past them at a distance of six feet. I avoid their eyes and I never look back.

And so I walk into Duruelo. No road runs through it. It is a rare haven of green. It dips and rises within a flat, brown world. It has small pastures, evergreen oaks and poplars. It has barns and it has pale cattle. A hand-painted sign indicates that they are 'Limusin'. Far away, I can see snow on the mountains beyond Ávila. Once this was a small village of some 20 families. Now it is less than that. It was here that Juan de Yepes, later Juan de la Cruz, John of the Cross, came in the winter of 1568 to set up a tiny priory, his first posting and the first priory for reformed friars in the whole over- ripe Carmelite Order. I am looking for the man and I am looking for his Spain, for which Juan's word was always not patria but tierra, his earth, his ground, just as his word for village was always pueblo, his people.

There are poppies blooming and I can hear cow bells. I drink from my hands at the spring that watered this hamlet for Juan and is now channelled through a stone headstone that resembles a family grave. In a niche there is a small, doll-sized statue of Juan. There are two quotations from his writings. 'Where there is not love put love and you will draw love out.' Difficult to improve on this as a mission for life. 'How well I know the spring which pours and runs although it is night'. All his life Juan looked to the darkness, literal and metaphorical. He believed that one must walk in darkness as the only way towards seeing a great light.

When Juan came to work in Duruelo he was just 26 years old. He had longed for a contemplative life, solitude and simplicity. 'I shall be better off among the stones than men.' Yet here he had been called to take the first step into a lifetime of ceaseless activity, involvement and complication. 'In order to arrive at what you are not you must go through what you are not.' So this man of stillness and purity set to busying himself in every lowly and messy, mundane necessity.

The first thing that struck people, on meeting Juan, was how small he was. I am eventually going to catch up with his bodily remains in the monastic cell in which he died, a long way from here. Those little bones give him a height of only 4 feet 10 inches, 147 centimetres. He may have been frail but he was always able to draw on a tenacious stamina. He may have been shy but he never lacked confidence or courage. First hand accounts of encounters with Juan have been gathered by the Carmelite teacher Crisógono de Jesús in his 'Vida de San Juan de la Cruz'. This book is the definitive chronicle, the spinal column of Juan's life story, onto which I try to put flesh and blood. In his landscape, in his poetry, in his time.

Juan looked out kindly from under well arched eyebrows. Sometimes it was an alert and intense glance, sometimes pensive and shaded. His skin was 'somewhat swarthy' a contemporary said. 'The colour of wheat' said others. Portraits showed an oval face with a broad forehead, dark hair always thinning, a slightly aquiline nose, a gentle expression. Another contemporary said that his modest presence was 'pleasing to look at'. It was a sweet look.

At times he had a bright and bird-like quickness about him, at times a stillness and bird-like poise. Sometimes he withdrew into an inner darkness, became absent, seemed to dream.

He loved darkness but he could not abide melancholy. He wanted to make sad people happy, sprinkling his conversation with amusing remarks and stories. He would lead one by the hand and not be parted until despondence had turned to cheerful optimism. But it was a caring delivered through smiles rather than laughter, and a joy often shared in solemnity. He was both sunshine and shade, sol y sombre, like Spain.

For the Spain of his time, he was a man of unusually deep and tender affection, with a feminine sensibility and insight into character. He was

5

patient, too. They said that he made a good companion. When they saw him coming down the road towards them, they felt happy.

As I snoop about Duruelo for vestiges of Juan's priory, I am taken in hand by a small, tough, friendly woman. She is wearing a rugby shirt, hooped dark red and blue. Today she has a distinctively red nose. With a sweep of her arm she invites me to look around me. 'Precioso', she says.

She leads me to a simple, single-storey white-painted chapel. This chapel now occupies the site of Juan's first, makeshift, little priory. We stand in it in silence for a few minutes.

Next she leads me into an adjoining two-storied house of brick. The shutters are all closed. But, once inside, we are in a small glassed-in cloister with radiators for winter and air-conditioning for summer. This is a convent for 16 Carmelite nuns. My guide tells me that if the number were ever to fall below a minimum complement of 15 the order would close it. So nuns are imported, mainly from Spain's old empire, to help keep the numbers up. Of course, we do not see them and we hear no voices or sounds of movement.

Outside again, my cheerful companion tells me that Juan was happier here than anywhere. She is all smiles too. I give her a 50 euro note for the convent funds. She gives me a small wooden cross made from oak that was watered by the spring that Juan and she, and I myself, have drunk from. A blue plastic bottle, filled from it, she forces on me. For I shall need it, she says, out there on the dry plain, away from Duruelo's oasis of green pastures and running waters.

I walk on towards Juan's birthplace, across the meseta, where the sun smites thee by day and the moon by night. This is the high, central table-land of Spain, nowhere below 1,500 feet. It's distances seem endless. The land is dusty, unfenced, unhedged, and trees are rare. The meseta is Old Castile at its most typical. Here I feel especially close to the past. The soil is poor, the climate is severe. Nine months of invierno, winter, three months of summer, inferno.

Spain is the most elevated country in Europe, after Switzerland. Great tracts of it are flat and high. The vast, raised Iberian interior is stretched out like an ox-hide. On it live boar and deer, hares and rabbits. Partridge is always on the menu. The wolves of Juan's time have gone up into the mountains but the vultures have come down onto the meseta.

Ortega y Gasset, the essayist, wrote with such feeling about this meseta in his 'Invertebrate Spain'. Land which is land and nothing else – land without verdure, yellow earth, red earth, silver earth – a naked landscape emphasised now and then by rows of tall black poplars. At times the plain rolls as if in torment and turns on itself to form gorges and ravines, sudden headlands and steep slopes. Under the sun's dreadful and despotic gaze the roads are pulverised, the leaves wither, the rivers dry up. In Castile there is four times as much evaporation as there is rain.

In Castile man lives in a town and goes to the country to work under the sun and under the hail. Then man escapes from the land and rests in the town. The land is empty, without habitation or human being for league on league. The countryside is mute, monotonous. Yet this very monotony, this quality of endlessness, is curiously exciting. It speaks of hardship and danger, of struggle and tenacity, of time and eternity, of life and death. This is a land of harsh, ascetic extremes. Castile does not compromise, and I love it.

It is also a world for the eye, an airy and unreal world which seems always on the point of vanishing. In Castile, the act of looking is like shooting an arrow at the infinite; neither on leaving the eye nor in the rest of its flight does it meet with any obstacle. When tired of flying through space, the arrow falls of its own weight and pierces a point in the earth which is almost a point in the sky. 'In Castile', said Ortega y Gasset, 'one sees better than anywhere else – but – one eats so badly!'

His friend, Antonio Machado, also wrote of Castile from the heart ('Campos de Castilla'):

> ... Oh, tierra triste y noble
> de los altos llanos y yermos y roquedas,
> de campos sin arades, regatos ni arboledas;
> decrépitas ciudades, caminos sin mesones,
> y antónitos palurdos sin danzas ni canciones!

> ... oh, sad and noble land,
> of the high plains, waste and stoney,
> of fields without ploughs, watercourses or groves;
> decrepit towns, roads without inns,
> and untuned folk without dances or songs!

It is a spare land.  This meseta produces men who are sparing of word and gesture.  No frills, no swagger.  There are only three things, the sun, the sky and the earth.  There is nothing to divert one.  Where the empty distances all around provide space for fear, man  learns to love his inner solitude as a defence.  The monotony of the landscape and man's searing exposure in it drive him into the refuge of his own inner shade.  Juan was a son of the meseta and he wrote:

> Olvido de lo criado,           Forgetting the creation,
> memoria del Criador,           remember the Creator,
> atención a lo interior         look to the interior
> y estarse amando al Almado.    and be loving to the Loved One

Walking the meseta in the tracks of Juan, I walk with double vision.  I see what I see – and in Castile one sees better than anywhere else – and I look for what Juan saw here too.

He saw then the landscape that I see now.  But Juan looked into this Spanish interior to see within it, simultaneously, a glorious, poetic vision of his own.  This trick of double vision is the Spanish religion, its most famous practitioner Don Quixote, who romanced these bare plains in the same years that Juan walked them.  I walk to try and get a look-in myself.

> Mas busca en tu espejo al otro,
> al otro que va contigo.
>
> But look in your mirror for the other,
> the other who goes with you together.
>                         Antonio Machado 1875-1939

# 2 BEGINNING IN FONTIVEROS

I walk into Fontiveros on a cool, grey morning. Here and there, from time to time, large raindrops fall in empty promise of more to come. I turn off the new road that now skirts the village. On the corner stand the petrol pumps of the Estación de Servicio San Juan de la Cruz.

The village is still shuttered up, but gradually awakening. Not much goes on here. the population has shrunk to an impoverished 1,000 souls from an impoverished 5,000 in Juan's day.

Fontiveros has always been a plain Castilian village without a watercourse right out on the great, dry meseta. Here at 2,900 feet above sea level, it stands in the middle of the almost treeless, almost featureless, 7,500 square kilometres of quadrilateral plateau whose corners are marked by the cities of Salamanca to the west, Medina del Campo to the north, Segovia to the east, and Avila to the south. Already, in June, the land is beginning to look scorched.

The largest building, set in an open space in the centre of the village, is the church. It is a fine church and it dominates the scene in a measured and dignified way, combining a spacious gravitas with the warmth of medieval brickwork. The rest is mean streets.

People are beginning to come out, a few on foot, fewer still in cars. Most of them seem to be dressed to match the surrounding meseta in variations of light brown, in rough wool, undyed cloth, hemp, canvas, sackcloth I suppose for work at ground level. These lean, gaunt men and women do not look cut out for leisure except possibly for that sport between villages that used to enliven a dead of winter's day: a presumed insult, then hostile stares, stones, fists, knives, group scrimmages, when football was in its infancy (Ruiz, 'Spanish Society 1400-1600').

Juan was born here in 1542. Spain was exactly 50 years old. In 1492 the ruling couple, the reyes católicos, Isabel of Castile and Ferdinand of Aragon, had put the last piece of the jigsaw into place with the capture of Granada from the Moors. Now Spain was the richest country in the world. But for the most part it didn't look it.

80% of Spain's people lived here in Castile, the great interior, known as Old Castile in its northern half and New Castile in its southern half. The rest, the people of the surrounding mountains and seashores, were looked upon by Castilians as somewhat peripheral, somewhat secondary Spaniards. Not serious. The language of Spain was Castilian. To speak Spanish was hablar Castillano.

Castilians lived in villages rather than in towns – at least most of them did. And most of them were the poor, the peasants, the petty artisans, the hired labourers. When day broke over Fontiveros they either walked out to work the land or sat down at home to weave cheap cloth.

The middle classes were thin on the ground out here. Those with education were more likely to take it with them into church, priory or convent than into local law, medicine or commerce. And they were outnumbered by the idle hidalgos. A hidalgo, hijo de algo, son of something (property, title), counted himself noble and was conveniently excused taxes. A hidalgo, a man with nothing to do, was proud of himself however few his acres, however run-down his homestead and however rusty his armour. Cervantes's 'old-fashioned gentleman' was an archetype, with his ancient shield on a shelf, his skinny nag and his greyhound, his housekeeper and his one man to serve both in house and field (Cervantes. 'The Life and Achievements of Don Quixote de la Mancha'). There was no getting away from him, one in every ten Castilians.

One evening in 1530 a well-connected young man, travelling on business, arrived in Fontiveros and found a lodging for the night. Gonzalo de Yepes had been brought up in the wealth of Toledo. Both his father and his mother had counted themselves noble, with property around Yepes, which is 30 kilometres east of Toledo, as well as a town house in the city itself. But they had died while Gonzalo was a child.

The extended family had then cared for him. His uncles seem to have been numerous and successful. Three were silk merchants. Four were canons of the cathedral. One was archdeacon of the collegiate church in nearby Torrijos.

An archdeacon, canons, silk merchants – these look like Jewish credentials in the Castile of that time. Many Jewish families who had converted to Christianity several generations earlier – from conviction, convenience or compulsion – had talents that thrived in church administration, commerce and finance. They were known as conversos to signal their 'otherness' from 'Old Christians of pure blood'. And where Old Christians looked down on work as a desperate last resort, conversos actually sought employment. But there had been much intermarriage. It was said that many Castilian men married Jewish wives for their sensuality, which the bone-hard Castilian women of the meseta lacked. And those bone-hard women secured for themselves converso husbands whose Jewish lineage had always provided excellent and hard-working craftsmen, merchants, financiers and intellectuals.

So Gonzalo, although an orphan, was well set up in his extended converso family, with a secure start in life. But it may have left a gap for love to fill.

Young Gonzalo was now old enough to travel for his uncles on business. They used to send him regularly, with their silken products, to represent them at the great market held in Medina del Campo. It was 170 kilometres north of Toledo, 30 leagues, two or three days on the road. Fontiveros was a convenient overnight stopping place. And there he set eyes on a handsome young village girl and fell in love.

Catalina Álvarez was, like Gonzalo, an orphan from Toledo. But the death of her parents had left her with nobody and nothing. She had to fend for herself alone in what were, anyway, hard times. Eventually she had found herself a bare living as a weaver in Fontiveros. She was a humble girl but resilient and she developed into a young woman with a sweet nature and a beauty rare in such coarse-grained surroundings. And she fell in love with Gonzalo de Yepes.

Did Gonzalo take Catalina to meet all those rich uncles and aunts in and around Toledo? Possibly, because later she would know where to look to seek help from them. But despite her sweet nature and her rare beauty, and despite Gonzalo pleading the cause of true love, not one of them would accept her and not one of them would agree to the match. She was an illiterate weaver. She had no connections and no dowry. If Gonzalo insisted on marrying beneath himself and his family he would be cut off with nothing, disowned, disinherited, stony broke.

Gonzalo sacrificed all for love. He lost every scrap of social standing. He was to start again from scratch with Catalina. They were married in

Fontiveros's great church. He was twenty and she was eighteen. Catalina set about teaching him to weave, with her, the cheap cloth that was their lifeline.

One barren year followed another in Castile, one poor harvest after another. Sometimes bread was not to be had for any money. Barley with lentils was the staple dish. Wood for cooking and warmth was scarce on the meseta.

Soon their first child, Francisco, was born, always a strong boy. He was their only child until he was about seven, when Luis arrived, who would be always sickly. Finally, four years later, into this small, windswept township of mud and tile and brick came Juan de Yepes, tiny, precious, new-born mystic, poet and saint. He was perhaps named for John the Baptist, perhaps born or baptised on that saint's name day, 24 June 1542.

But their father, Gonzalo, still only thirty-three years of age when Juan was born, was already ailing. In fact he was already dying of hard work, poor sustenance and the anguish of the struggle to do better for his little family. Briefly they matched the standard Castilian household unit, a nuclear family of two adults and three children. Then, either in Juan's first winter or his second, his father died. Juan, so young, would not be able to carry any memory of him forward into his life.

The courage to make one's own way, the resilience of the reed that may be bent by the storm but will not break, and above all a life centred on love, these were the qualities of Gonzalo, and of Catalina. They would become the essence of Juan.

Catalina was now struggling alone to provide for four mouths. When spring came, desperate for help, she set out to tackle Gonzalo's rich family around Toledo. Strong Francisco, about thirteen, and the sickly Luis, about seven, would have to walk beside her. Little two-year Juan had to be carried. There were 150 kilometres of track and waste and mountain to overcome, to reach the nearest uncle, in Torrijos. Through San Pedro de Arroyo, Ávila, over the pass to Barraco, Cebreros, the green road past the great stone toros de Guisando, up again to Cadalso de los Vidrios and down to Escalona. When I walk this path I stop in simple inns with basic facilities. For Catalina these were miserable looking hovels where travellers slept on the ground in yards and stables and kitchens. Not that most of them provided food. Catalina must have had to beg for food for her children along the way.

And so they came to the friendly, four-square town of Torrijos and to the magnificently ornate stone arch that frames the door of the collegiate church. Its steps provided a fitting stage for the encounter. The young mother who brought with her her whole equity, which was only love, pleaded at the door of the religious institution which, over centuries, had elaborated its first principle which, too, was only love. And the greatest of these is charity. The church, the archdeacon, the uncle, denied them love, turned them away and closed the door on them.

| Del verbo divino | With the divine Word |
| la Virgen preñada | pregnant comes the Virgin |
| viene de camino | along the path |
| si le dais posada. | if you will take her in. |

Juan wrote these lines many years later when he himself was a churchman. Perhaps they resonated in him with his mother's rejection in Torrijos. The family had denied her existence, and his.

Back home she went on the long hard road to endless weaving to provide for her boys in the cramped little house in Fontiveros. Soon the next blow fell. Luis died. He was eight. That he was buried under a slab beside his father in the nave of the great church suggests a certain respect for this struggling household, at least in Fontiveros if not in Toledo.

The following year, within a few feet of the bodies of his father and his brother, Juan began to be schooled in his catechism. Here a life-sized crucifixion looked down from a side-chapel onto the little converso. With its lean, twisted body, the face of a nomad and a skin colour between dirty olive and pewter, it had come to be known as 'the Semite Christ'.

In this very same year that Juan started to learn his catechism, anti-semitism was given a new momentum. The Archbishop of Toledo drew up the statutes of purity of blood, limpieza de sangre. His converso canons, the de Yepes men among them resisted impotently. Gainful ecclesiastical posts were now going to be closed to conversos unless they could prove purity of bloodline for the last four generations. And the same thing would apply to organisations of nobles, to the military, to confraternities, corporations and professional bodies, and even to hospitals. There were frantic investigations. The roads of Castile were infested with commissars looking for information, searching local archives, interrogating the very old for their memories (Bennassar. 'L'Homme Espagnol').

Only Old Christians could claim that descent from the Visigoths conferred on them nobility. Even Sancho Panza claimed that it gave him the right to be a duke, for, 'Though poor, I am an Old Christian and owe nothing to anybody'. And, at street level, it was the smell of cooking with olive oil rather than with pork fat that was said to betray a converso family – 'the smell of the Jews'.

There was no longer a living to be had for Catalina and her boys in Fontiveros, its subsistence economy already in decline. They would try their luck in Arévalo, whose main virtue, for them was that, although no more flourishing than Fontiveros, it was twice as big. Catalina left the little home she had set up with her husband, where she had given birth to three babies, and where she had closed the eyes of Gonzalo and young Luis. She left them in their graves and, carrying all that could be managed between them, she, Francisco and six-year-old Juan set out across five leagues of the meseta, five hours, towards life in Arévalo. It must have been a sad walk.

Before I follow them, I take a look around the village of Fontiveros. I search for Catalina's house in a street now called Calle Carmen. It used to be called Calle Cantiveros as it was the most direct route to the neighbouring village of that name, one league away, before the new road came. There are small, two-storied houses. Quite shortly Calle Carmen opens onto the empty plain.

Two village ladies take me in hand. We discuss Juan in my awkward Castilian. They lead me to a Carmelite Convent. It was here when Juan was here, but has since been grandly rebuilt. They want me to try the closed door because, they say, I shall be able to buy recuerdos, souvenirs, inside. I hang back and they seem nervous to try the door themselves.

Nearby I find a small, brick church. In a niche it has a statue of the saintly Juan, enrobed and spreading his hands in a pope-like blessing. There is also a plaque commemorating 350 years from Juan's birth, 24 junio 1542-

24 junio 1892. This church occupies the site of Catalina's little house, Juan's first home. I am sorry not to be able to see that. And the church is locked.

In the centre of Fontiveros I find a gigantic statue of Juan raised up high on a triumphalist stone plinth. What kind of impression of their local saint can this possibly give the children of the village? The converso child, the little friar and prior, the poet, the mystic, the quiet rebel in the cause of love, all hid from sight by this posthumous hero in cast-iron who brandishes a mighty iron cross and wears a great, round iron halo on the back of his head. The whole set-up looks like a war memorial. It bears an incongruous slogan: 'Lord to suffer and to be despised for you'. Indeed.

Around the church there are children playing. There is another cross, in concrete. The inscription says that it was 'destroyed by Marxism in 1932 and restored in 1941'.

Two of the children produce a key and unlock the church door. Catholic priests always seem to be assisted at every hand's turn by children. These children have faces designed by Breughel and Goya. Three of them will me towards a coin-operated electric device near 'the Semite Christ'. The prayer that it illuminates is that I myself may become the fire to burn up within me my own selfishness, pride, impurity: el egoismo, orgullo, impureza. Which is what would happen, I suppose, if I were an Inquisition penitent burning at the stake in my own auto de fe, my act of faith.

The bells in the tower above clang for mass, each at its own pace. Little Juan must have been summoned by this same rhythmic chaos.

I follow Catalina and the boys on foot, north-east, out of the village. The houses on either side of the street get smaller and smaller. Not much sign, any more, of the gambling dens and brothels of itinerant prostitutes that some of them probably housed when Juan walked by (Ruiz again). Perhaps not much demand, any more, with today's diminished population. And even fewer travellers like me wandering through.

The village ends abruptly. Not far out I pass a reedy pond. Was this the pond Juan fell in? He told the story of it at least twice to fellow Carmelites after he grew up. He was playing with other children beside this pond.

They were throwing sticks down vertically into the water, like spears, and snatching them as they bobbed up again. But Juan lost his balance and plunged in headfirst, his hands reaching down to the muddy bottom. He came up for an instant but sank again, and seemed to see a beautiful lady above him, reaching out her hand for his own. Juan, the little converso child, would not take her fine white hand in his own muddy one for fear of defiling it. But the other children had called a passing labourer who hooked Juan's shirt with his goad and hoisted him out. In this same year that Juan saw a beautiful lady where the water of a muddy pool was churned up, was born the chronicler of Spanish double vision, Cervantes.

After the pond there are only spreads of ripening wheat, or barley, or oats. There is an occasional square of untilled dust and weeds. The trees are few and far between, and small. Every league or so a primitive hamlet, just cottages and a church among farm buildings, closed doors and shutters, no commerce. Often the road simply misses the place. Away from these villages there are no isolated farmsteads, only the odd lichen-covered cross of stone or concrete. Twice there are stretches of rough grass where antique flocks of sheep graze, guarded by man and dog.

The earth's flat skyline is so far away I can barely make it out. I see an occasional harrier, a buzzard, a kite. Mostly, no vehicles on the road. Mostly, in any one league, there is nothing to look at. Nothing. Nada. Appropriately, nada is what Juan will come to insist on as the necessary first stage in a spiritual journey. No reflex to the world around. No reflex to the world within. No awareness of self in time and space. Oblivious. This is the step into the dark that the adult Juan will teach as nada, the first step to todo. To everything. Sombre that will reveal sol. The darkness that will reveal the light.

Walking through the five leagues of this landscape, five hours as just a shadow under the sun, should be a fine way to induce nada. But I am too aware of myself and my sore feet to be able to become so detached.

I wonder how six-year old Juan managed this walk. Perhaps the amiable Francisco carried him from time to time. Later, Juan warned allegorically: 'Even if the path is flat and smooth for men of good will, he who walks it will make much effort and not go far if he does not keep his feet and his spirit in good order and persist bravely in the same'. No reason why a boy can't give a man such a lesson.

As I hobble into the outskirts of Arévalo an old lady takes me in hand to guide me. I need someone to guide me but I am not clear about her offer, so I several times limp rudely ahead. Each time she catches me at the next road crossing. Finally she delivers me into the centre of the town.

# 3  MUDDLING THROUGH IN ARÉVALO

I wander around in the muddle that is Arévalo and I wonder what Juan saw in it. And how it helped shape him. For it was already a muddle then.

Arévalo says of itself that the origin of the city is an unresolved mystery. And, more mysteriously, 'Nowadays Arévalo has a population of 7,800 inhabitants registered in the census but its real population is over 10,000 inhabitants'. So nearly a quarter are passing through like me. In 1548, the de Yepes family joined just such a shifting and uncertain crowd.

Arévalo had seen better times. The Castilian Parliament was no longer making frequent visits to meet in the Royal Palace, which itself was no longer functioning as a Royal Palace. And the grim castle, the prow of the walled town where its two rivers meet, was no longer a fortress but a prison for distressed hidalgos. Arévalo had been a bench mark for Castilian architecture in brick. Its bricks were crumbling.

But it was still a centre of cloth weaving. And it had a large converso population. For Catalina, there might be work to be had and support to be found. Why not a second husband? She was 37. But she didn't look for marriage. Perhaps she had enough loving to do with her two boys.

Straightaway she looked for work, and she found it, for herself and Francisco. They weaved in a small workshop. Its owner paid them, day by day, for what they produced. It was probably poor stuff. By now, most of the good merino wool was being exported. In Castile there was little concern for craft or quality. Its cloth was becoming less and less competitive in the great markets. Wages had peaked and were about to start falling, year by year, for a whole decade. Growth in the economy was just running out. Inflation was setting in. The poor earned money to survive from one day to the next, not to secure the future.(Pérez, 'L'Espagne du XVI$^e$ Siècle')

Catalina also managed to find somewhere to live. In town, artisans' houses were like little bird cages, narrow, one room deep, with a ladder to an upper level. They were lit by an open front door and access to a tiny yard at the back. (Casey 'Early Modern Spain')

Often the family must have gone to bed hungry. At best they ate dark rye bread and drank water conditioned with sharp, local wine. At best, from time to time, some mutton or pork, more often salted than fresh. At best a smattering of vegetables.

Nearby, I walk across an open space, the blank footprint of the once Royal Palace. There are pretty girls around and formidable ladies. It strikes me that the dark gene that has come up into Castile from the south, Moorish and Semitic, shows up more in women than in men and more in middle-age than in youth. These are true heads of families, these are Spanish battle-axes.

I find that the Tourist Office has been removed from its central, advertised location to a cupboard full of pamphlets in a church. Two men oversee the cupboard, an optimist and a pessimist, whom I think of as Sol and Sombre. While Sol gives me cheerful advice, Sombre seems to have pocketed my pen.

I am directed by them to the Plaza San Pedro. I walk around in this square where Catalina and her boys lived. Now there are stunted plane trees and graffiti. There is a plastic bus shelter. Mean, two-storied houses have replaced earlier mean, two-storied houses. But somehow this shabby square, its lie of the land, feels not a bad place to live. Catalina, Francisco and Juan must have felt some happiness together here.

From the square I walk down a narrow street 100 yards to where it opens out onto the castle, a grand block of blank walls, windowless. In its darkness, the mother of the Isabel of Castile who drove the Moors from Spain was shut away to go mad, and much of her daughter's childhood was shut away here with her too. It looks to me like a gloomy neighbour for little Juan. Perhaps he saw in it a more chivalric, crusading identity.

At the other end, the street passes through an arcade right under the bell tower of the handsome, brick church of Santa Maria, the parish church of the de Yepes. Every evening, as darkness fell, Juan listened to the bell of Santa Maria toll 100 times. Perhaps he counted. It tolled to warn of the closing of the town gates, for the town was defined by its walls. But, to the six-year-old, it might have seemed to toll for him.

What had Juan been doing all day while Catalina and Francisco were at their looms? He was at an age at which it was believed important to inculcate good orthodox religious doctrines and moral customs. He would be expected to be able to read by now. Was he at school? Local councils of Castilian towns, and private individuals, would put aside rents and revenues to organise rudimentary public elementary schools. And the Jesuits had just started to establish their own free schools. Somehow a willing and resourceful little boy, and a boy of vision, must have found his way into some sort of education. Perhaps the parish priest helped.

And what an eye-opener Arévalo itself must have been for Juan after sleepy Fontiveros. Here all was noise and bustle. Society was in the melting pot. Arévalo, on the trade routes between Madrid, Salamanca, Ávila, Segovia, Valladolid and Medina, was a filter that collected much of the itinerant dross. Here were thieves, fraudsters, parasites, vagabonds, fallen women. The destitute were on every corner: old widows, abandoned children, cripples. And around every corner violence was possible. Disdain for work in the Castilian role model, the hidalgo class, was mimicked in the posturing of picaros, rogues and villains. Vagrants would switch from begging to banditry and back again. Prostitution was good business and well ordered. The women were required to go to mass once a week and to the surgeon once a month. Syphilis was just now becoming a scourge in Old Castile.

Casey's 'Early Modern Spain' and Elliott's 'Imperial Spain' describe just how hard these times were.

Tides of bubonic plague, smallpox, diphtheria and lethal influenza swept across Spain's heartland. Death was familiar. And for the common people who yet lived there were lesser infections, skin diseases, lice and falling teeth. And they lived, always, on the edge of hunger, for droughts and famine racked Old Castile. Juan observed all this.

Juan saw people crowding into Arévalo who were less and less able to find regular means of subsistence. Begging was a growth industry and the authorities had to try and institutionalise it. One must get a begging licence from one's parish priest, if one was unable to provide for oneself through labour. It was valid only up to six leagues from one's place of birth or residence, except in times of famine. Children over the age of five were not to accompany begging parents. Only the blind did not need a licence. Penalties for unauthorised begging were 60 lashes, imprisonment, the galleys or exile. Compliance with the law was administered by the town corregodor, a crown appointment for a hidalgo who could be bothered to work, if one could be found. (Martz 'Poverty and Welfare in Habsburg Spain')

Juan will have learnt of the attempts of the rich to save, or at least to improve, the poor through stern benevolence. Titled lords, merchants, prelates, professionals were setting up houses of assistance, hospitals, soup kitchens. From monastery to monastery wandered vagrants in search of bread.

For three years all this seethed around the little boy. It must have given him much food for thought. He knew that, in three generations of his own direct family, all four grandparents, his father and one brother had already died – all young – while only his mother, one brother and he himself lived on. Who had the time to talk it through with him as he looked for some insight into the street scene? Perhaps only the watercarrier trading at the crossroads with his barrel and cups. Juan's crossroads are still there for me to walk by but the watercarriers have gone.

This was one of the critical moments of Juan's development. The age of seven brings the first climacteric, the first great transition, physical, psychological and social. Until this point the infant has been a dependent satellite of an adult or adults, not self-sustaining. At seven the child becomes 'viable', able to survive independently beyond the domestic hearth, if necessary to survive as an urchin on the streets of Rio de Janeiro, Calcutta or even Arévalo. For Juan this was a time of change, of maturation, of looking forward. It could influence the course his life would take.

What about Francisco? What effect was Arévalo, and his growing up there, having on him? He was still a good fellow. How could he not be in Catalina's care? He was still kindly, gentle and fun. He was unable to read or write, but he was good with his hands, and he could sing, dance and play the guitar. For a little while he became rather wild and would wander the streets late at night with noisy groups of friends. He was, after all, eighteen.

On some nights Francisco and his friends would even stay outside the city walls until dawn, raiding orchards, vineyards and fields. This was an additional burden that the poor peasants who farmed the land around could well have done without. Droughts and blights had been racking Old Castile. A man had to divide his land in two and work it año y vez, year and turn, one half always fallow. The work was hard and taxation was becoming heavier and heavier. Rent absorbed half his harvest (Ruiz). And then there was the Mesta to dread. The Mesta was a royally approved organisation of sheep owners associations which supervised and controlled the twice-yearly movement of three and a half million sheep right across the middle of Castile. Towards October the herds left the green slopes and foothills in the north, to flock southward and winter in the warmer margins. They travelled at two to four leagues per day. The cañada, the sheepwalk, was uncultivated to forty paces either side of the road. Whenever one saw a great cloud of dust moving across the fields it was made by these flocks of sheep. Don Quixote saw an army in such a cloud of dust, led by many knights, and he charged the sheep fearlessly. But struggling peasants simply had to let the Mesta do sometimes dreadful damage to their meagre crops.

If, despite the worst that drought, disease and the Mesta could do, the peasant bought his efforts to fruition, he could enjoy a short summer joy of harvest, vendange and fruit picking. Into this, one summer's night, Francisco and his friends brought mischief. They picked and ate their fill and laid waste to much more.

This was a turning point for Francisco. Once home, he felt terrible remorse. He went and sought out the parish priest, and together they talked through the nature and the depth of his repentance. For some time, he would return to the priest each evening after work, for Christian teaching. And then, one night, on an impulse, he picked up a destitute wretch from the church steps and carried him home, to wash, feed and shelter him. This was the start of a lifetime of such attentions. What an additional burden it must have been for Catalina, as Francisco brought the helpless sufferers into their tiny home. But how she must have loved her son in the good work.

And what an impression his elder brother's kindness to strangers must have made on Juan.

Now there was another positive milestone in Francisco's life. He met a girl called Ana Izquierdo (this name is a Basque word for left-handed). Ana lived about three leagues out of Arévalo. Her father was a peasant smallholder. Ana would bring the produce into town to sell in the market, where Francisco courted her. Soon he brought her home to meet Catalina and Juan. Next it was arranged that she should spend time with them learning to weave. Francisco and Ana married. She and Catalina became devoted to each other too. She took on the care of Francisco's waifs and strays with as much loving kindness as the rest of the family did. So now they were four.

They had been three years in Arévalo. It's continuing chaotic decline was dragging them down. They could no longer make a living. They had to move on to somewhere where the market for their humble skill was wider and better structured. They had to go and take their chances in Medina del Campo, only six leagues to the north-west. So once again they packed up everything they could carry and took to the road across the meseta.

I follow them away from Arévalo, but my first staging post is the Tourist Office cupboard again. I have a problem with the road to Medina del Campo. The old road, the one that the de Yepes family probably walked, now has the Autovia Madrid-Coruña on top of it. Sol assures me that there is a tiny camino for walkers that runs along beside the hard shoulder of this motorway, but he can guarantee it only for the first ten kilometres. Sombre writes down for me, with my ex-pen, the name of a hostel which later turns out not to exist. I decide to follow a dog-leg route in order to avoid the motorway. This will increase the distance to 55 kilometres, ten leagues, ten hours walking, two days rather than one since my pack is heavy.

My lesser road takes me across a bridge and I am immediately in the countryside. The town's walls are porous. There is an intimacy here between the urban and the rural. The road now is straight and, to my surprise, the first league is gently uphill. I am surprised because Arévalo had declared itself to me as the highest urban centre on the meseta. Also a surprise are some woods and banks of wild flowers. Then I pass through an insignificant village called Aldeaseca - dry village - and the meseta soon reverts to type: earth, sky and sun, monotonous, pitiless, endless.

Too sharp a consciousness of my own feet prevents me walking into that state of un-awareness of self in time and space which Juan recommended as the pursuit of nada, nothingness. So I resort to counting my blessings and thus come happily, in the afternoon, to Madrigal de las Altas Torres.

Madrigal is a small town. The whole of it is enclosed within a circular defensive wall, most of which is still standing. It is less than half a mile across. The name sounds lyrical but originally meant not a song for voices in the mother tongue but, rather, a tangle of bushes and briars. (Trend, 'The Language and History of Spain'). The high towers must have been added later.

The town is very quiet. The streets are not tarred or paved since there is no traffic. A rare passer-by hugs the wall, avoids the open spaces. I manage a conversation with an old man. He tells me that Juan was never here. True perhaps for Juan the boy but not necessarily so for Juan the man. He might have come this way when walking to university in Salamanca, or to take up his first posting at Duruelo. It is quite difficult to miss Madrigal in this empty plain.

I find the tourist office. It is closed. The churches are locked. I find the museum in the small palace in which Isabel was born. Like Don Quixote she is all over Castile. The notice of opening hours suggests that the museum is open, but the door is locked. I knock and wait, and knock again. Eventually a woman's voice berates me shrilly from within.

I sit down in the shade and find my pen in a little used pocket. Poor Sombre was unfortunate enough to have an identical one and I have mistakenly condemned him as a whole man, just for his pen. I need to get closer to Juan, for him to keep me out of such mischief. Even as a nine-year-old on the road to Medina del Campo he could already have reminded me, 'He that loves not his neighbour abhors God'. At a later age he would develop the argument that if we persist in trying to judge the world through putting together two of our own fallibilities –first our so-called 'natural knowledge' (what we fancy we see and hear) and then our flawed reasoning ability applied to it – we subject ourselves to falsehoods, imperfections, desires, opinions and wastes of time. It's obvious really. Better to keep one's mind open. Or, Juan would say, better to keep one's soul in the dark, detached, unjudgemental, quiet, nothing, nada, leaving room there for love.

The long straight road towards Medina del Campo continues the next morning. Pan, vino y ajo crudo hacen andar el viejito agudo – bread, wine and raw garlic make the old boy walk sharp. At first I hear hoopoes and see bursts of wild flowers in the ditches, but, as the heat increases, the landscape settles into its true meseta emptiness. I pass signposts to villages surnamed Matacabras – goatkillers. In one called Fuente el Sol, the sun spring, I drink beer.

When I reach town I see that its river, the Zapardiel, is dry. Its source is only 60 kilometres away, but, in early summer, its waters have all evaporated before they reach Medina del Campo.

When Catalina, Francisco and Ana, and Juan arrived here the Zapardiel was full. A fish jumped. Juan saw a monstrous fish about to hurl itself on him. Terrified, he made the sign of the cross and it plunged back into the depths. This was his second strange, watery encounter.

# 4   COMING OF AGE IN MEDINA DEL CAMPO

I find that I really like Medina del Campo.  I like its simple name, 'the town of the countryside'.  Everyone I meet is friendly and helpful to me.  Something of Juan must have rubbed off on Medina.  And something of Medina must have rubbed off on Juan too, since he arrived here when he was only nine and did not leave until he was twenty-two.  The place in which one spends one's teenage years is the place, above all, that one knows most intimately.  For Juan, a quarter of his life would be spent here.

Today, Medina del Campo is once again a good place to have as a hometown.  In the nineteenth century it went through a disastrous ghost town phase, abandoned by its population, all but a couple of thousand of them.  Now it is born again and 20,000 people live here.  Most of the buildings have been replaced, but there are still some fine old ones around and there is still plenty of brick.  And nobody has tried to improve on the comfortable medieval layout of streets and squares.  Its prosperity now is based on agriculture and, strangely, on the wood transformation industry.  Strange, in that there are so few trees out there on the surrounding meseta.

In Juan's time there were twice as many people crammed into the town as there are now.  They lived here because, twice a year, in May and October, Medina del Campo was host to the greatest market of Castile, 'The General Fair of the Kingdom'. Merchants came from all over Spain, from Flanders, Naples, Genoa, France, England, and from 'the Indies'.  Each trade had its allotted pitch.  Every street and square was used, and the lines of stalls stretched right up to the castle on the hill (Casey).

The great arsenal of Castile, Castillo de la Mota had been presented to Isabel.  So here she was again, and here she had chosen to die, 50 years before Juan arrived, in a modest house built over an arch in the corner of the Plaza Mayor.  Or, as some people said, she died in the castle, as that was where her coffin set out from on its three-week December journey, in apocalyptic storms, to its grave in Granada.  Juan would come to know that long trail well, and I too.

Catalina and her family arrived in hope sometime in 1551.  Evidently it was not during the meseta's three months of inferno since there was enough water in the river for a fish to jump from it.

Somehow they found a lodging similar to what they had left in Arévalo, one up and one down with a yard at the back. Here they set up their looms. Now they were weaving a mixture of cotton and worsted, or cotton and silk when they could afford it: bombasine. Burato, they called it then and it was usually in black and much used for mourning. In more cheerful fashion they also wove the same materials into coifs, cheap head coverings for everyday wear, or even for the fair. Three looms, Catalina, Francisco and Ana working them, Juan in and out on errands, cooking, eating, sleeping, all had to be fitted into the tiny space, day and night. And Ana was soon to be pregnant.

Fortunately they were able to move Juan out. A little further up their street, on the same side, a small boarding school had been set up. Colegios de la Doctrina, or, as they were familiarly known, los niños de la doctrina – the boys of the teaching – were being set up in cities all over Castile. They might be funded by local benefactors but they were overseen by the municipal authorities. In this case, the noble knight don Rodrigo de Dueñas lived in a magnificent palace just across the road and he it was who funded the school.

The colegios were principally intended for orphans but other very poor boys were also accepted up to the age of 10. So Juan was taken in, housed, clothed in a uniform, fed and taught. He would be here for five years, at a boarding school just 150 yards from home. He must have been able to keep in close touch with his family,

The education concentrated on the basics; by copying, memorisation and repetition they learnt Christian doctrine, moral texts, Latin grammar and numeracy. In Juan's first year the church in Spain banned the reading of the scriptures in Spanish. But Juan's Latin would have kept him up to a mark above the zone policed by the dreaded cane of the priest who taught them.

In return for their schooling the poor boys had certain obligations to fulfil. Juan was one of four who worked in the sacristy of the church of the convent of Santa Maria Magdalena, just next door and also funded by the great don Rodrigo across the road. They were on duty in the sacristy from six until ten in the morning during the summer and from seven until eleven during the winter. They had to keep the church clean and all the vestments in order, to assist in services and generally to be on call as needed by sacristan, chaplain and nuns. There was probably some time for larking about. The nuns loved Juan, Crisógono de Jesús says.

Another obligation, for all the pupils, was to embellish funerals. They would wear black, carry banners, process solemnly and sing.

As they had all been accepted on the basis of their poverty and inability to get onto the first rung of any ladder towards a decent livelihood, the colegio also tried to turn them into artisans. It could not teach them trades itself but it could use its influence to obtain part-time apprenticeships for them. Juan was sent out to work for a carpenter, who found the little boy an unsatisfactory assistant and returned him. The same thing happened with a wood carver. Next he failed at painting and decorating. And finally tailoring. Unlike his elder brother he just wasn't good with his hands. But he did look very small and sweet, so he was entrusted with going out into the streets and appealing for alms for the orphans who were his fellow-pupils. In this he succeeded.

I walk the street that Juan lived in, learnt in and served in. It starts from the corner of the great square, the Plaza Mayor. This is a spacious square but the buildings around it are not very high and there are trees in it, so it is not so grand and formal as the Plaza Mayor one finds in many a Castilian town. From the square Juan's narrow street runs north-west to the Santiago gate in the walls – gate and walls now long since quarried entirely away for the rebuilding of Medina.

Halfway along the street, after some 300 yards, I come to the site of Catalina's little house, on the left. There is now a long, two storied, brick building here, very neat and symmetrical with its straight rows of rectangular, barred windows on each floor. I decide, on no grounds whatsoever, that Catalina's house was probably at the point at which there is now a hard, rubber speed-bump fixed across the road. I regret not being able to see the original, sixteenth century dwelling.

I head on up the street, past a traffic sign showing two small children running. So there are still children in this street. After a further 150 yards, I come to a great studded, wooden door set in a brick wall on the left. Above it a plaque says, 'Monasterio Santa Maria Magdalena M M Agustinas'. This door opens into a yard from which one can enter the church in which Juan worked as a sacristy boy. This monasterio is still an Augustinian nunnery.

At eight o'clock in the evening, I am back here for mass. The church is packed. A row of tall iron bars right across the church near the back closes off about one quarter of its space. In this enclosure sit some 20 serious nuns in black, some very old, some just old, some young, one or two very young. One old one plays an organ. I take my place with my back to the bars through which the nuns used to watch Juan going about his work in this church.

When the time comes for 'the peace', the shaking of hands with one's neighbour, some of the congregation turn and smile and wave to the nuns. Family and friends, perhaps,. I half turn and half smile, awkwardly, avoiding catching any particular nun's eye. For communion, the priest marches right down the aisle to feed the nuns through the bars.

Outside in the street, there are graffiti on the wall. Faszistes ignorames! Ni guerra entre pueblos ni paz entre clases! Accidente laboral-terrorismo patronal! Ignorant fascists! No war between peoples no peace between classes! Worker's accident – boss's terrorism!

At the end of the street, another 150 yards away, stands the great parochial church of the parish that the de Yepes family lived in, the church of Santiago, St James disciple of Jesus and patron saint of Spain. The church was actually completed while Juan was living in Medina, and was at that time known as San Pablo y San Pedro. The street was later named Calle Santiago. Now is has been renamed Calle de Santa Teresa de Jesus, after the woman who changed Juan's life.

When I find it the church is locked, like so many Spanish churches. A young priest turns up and explains that it is locked to protect the patrimonio from robos. He wonders whether in England's unlocked churches there is not so much patrimonio at risk. He is probably right. Then he kindly takes me on a guided tour. There is only one image of Santiago himself in the church. He is in his role of matamoros, moorslayer, on his white horse. Severed Moorish heads roll about underfoot.

After Juan had been at school in Calle Santiago for a couple of years, and was aged about 12, he was out playing with some of the other boys one day when he fell down a well. Was he pushed? Was he such a good boy that he was getting on the others' nerves? Perhaps there was a push and the consequence went further than the intention. The well had only a low coping round it and Juan went down. It was a very deep well, a long drop, and he disappeared under the black water. The boys were scared but Juan bobbed up and called for a rope. They hauled him out. Passers by gathered and heard him describing how the Virgin Mary had appeared above the surface of the water in the dark well-shaft, and how she had reached out her hand to him and held him from sinking. This was Juan's third strange encounter of the watery kind. The story of it was quickly around the town and it was spoken of by some people as a miracle. The little boy became something of a celebrity.

Three years later Calle Santiago played host to the emperor,. A plague of locusts was ravaging Castile and the court was on the move. Charles V stayed with the generous don Rodrigo in his Palacio de los Dueñas, right opposite Santa Maria Magdalena and Juan's school. Juan must have seen the pomp and ceremony of his arrival and departure.

I walk back down Calle Santiago to the palace. It is an educational centre now and I am able to peer into its beautiful, airy courtyard, delicately colonaded and arched at ground and first floor levels. A turret rises above. There is no-one there.

It was time for Juan to leave Calle Santiago. He had learnt all there was to be learnt at the little school. He left it with a reputation as a good scholar and a selfless server who had been associated with some sort of possibly miraculous incident.

So he was taken in to work at one of Medina's fourteen hospitals. This was the hospital of Nuestra Señora de la Concepción, popularly known as the Hospital de Bubas. A buba was an inflamed swelling in glandular parts of the body, especially the groin or armpits. So this was the hospital for painful lumps and bumps, life-threatening blains and bulges. More often than not its patients simply turned out to have the plague. Others might be leprous or syphilitic. Juan washed and fed and nursed the sick and dying. He also acted as the hospital's messenger. And he continued to gather alms in the streets, for this was a charitable enterprise.

Providing intimate care for people dying in pain and putrefaction, without benefit of modern palliative treatment, must have been demanding for a sixteen-year old. And there was always the risk of becoming infected himself. But he saw more danger to his spiritual health than to his physical health. He must not let the consolation he found in good works in this world divert him from loving attention to the eternal mystery that is God in heaven. Juan came to believe that the works which one finds least fulfilling, most mortifying, and at which one is least proficient, are the most precious in the sight of God. And one must hide them not only from others but from oneself. Let not your left hand know what your right hand is doing. Don't think about it. Just do it.

Juan lived in the hospital, among the bodies with bubas, and worked for nothing but his bed and board. There wasn't much for staff or patients to eat that first year as there was again famine in Castile. Juan developed an uncomplicated approach to nursing which he would continue to put into practice for the rest of his life when caring for the sick. Find love in yourself for the sufferers and don't hide it. Have infinite patience with them. Do your utmost to keep them in good spirits.

Where was the Hospital de Bubas? It is nowhere to be seen now. People are ready to help me. A workman painting a wrought iron gate green directs me all over the place. A suave gentleman with a pointed grey beard, in the Museo de Ferias, talks me through an excellent, mud-brown maquette of the town in the sixteenth century. A dark girl in the Tourist Office fetches dusty, old, long-neglected tomes from the back office, which she helps me search through.

Along one side of the Plaza de San Agustin, on the western edge of the old town, runs a brick wall which looks old, but probably not old enough. There are empty door and window apertures in it through which I look at a large, dusty patch of waste ground. A crane stands at the ready beside it. This was where the Hospital de Bubas was, where young Juan nursed the sick and dying. It is on the line of the vanished city walls. Perhaps it had to be just outside.

Nearby, I come across a statue of the adult Juan. It is a warm terracotta statue of a real man, with his own distinctive looks and with an interested, concerned, perceptive expression on his face. This is not the cast-iron super-saint portrayed in Fontiveros, for which I am grateful. This feels more like the real Juan. So real that it almost runs the risk of looking slightly comical.

While Juan was working at the hospital, his brother Francisco kept up his own good works when he could make time away from his loom and his family. He specialised in rescuing foundlings from the doorsteps of the churches of Medina, infants abandoned for reasons of illegitimacy or poverty. He would clean them up, feed them and have them baptised, often standing godfather himself, before finding foster mothers for them and collecting alms to support them.

There was a cruel irony in this activity since, during these years in Medina, Francisco's wife Ana gave birth to seven baby boys and one after another they died in infancy. One little girl, named Ana like her mother, survived.

Catalina de Yepes wove on. Her products were made of lesser cloths, paños menores. Fine textiles were sold on stalls in the Plaza Mayor. Lesser cloths were sold in a lesser square, quite close to Catalina's house, now called Plazuela de Federico Velasco.

I find the square has been rebuilt in brick and concrete and has a playground for little children in it, shaded by trees.

Back at the Hospital de Bubas Juan decided, after nearly two years, to resume his studies. From his mother's house he walked out once again, along Calle Santiago, past the nunnery and church of Santa Maria Magdalena on the left, with his old school attached to it, past the Palacio of don Rodrigo on his right, and on to the end at the gate of Santiago, with the parish church beside it. On the other side of the church stood his new college, which he would attend part-time while carrying on at the hospital.

For more than ten years, the Jesuits had been establishing their own colleges across Castile, with free instruction in literacy and Latin (Kagan 'Students and Society in Early Modern Spain'). This was one. It had quickly become the cultural centre of Medina. The Jesuit fathers gave formal, highly structured lessons and held public academic functions. They also put on performances of plays. It was a college participating in the full flowering of humanist enthusiasm, albeit brief, in Spain. The teaching was stimulating and highly effective. There were three hours of classes each morning and three each afternoon, but Juan could not spend so much time away from his voluntary duties with the bubas. So he compensated by studying alone at all hours of the night. Was this where he became committed to the value of darkness? He worked at his books by the glimmer of an oil lamp in the hospital wood shed.

In four years with the Jesuits, Juan became saturated with Latin and Greek, logic and grammar, rhetoric and philosophy, history and literature. He read and read – the early fathers, the doctors of the church, the Latin greats, the Bible of course, Seneca. And then there was exposure to the new Spanish writings, the plays, the poetry, the romans picaresques. And contact and exchange of ideas with professors and fellow students, debates, arguments.

When he left the college after four years Juan had flowered. He had reached his second climacteric, the age of twenty-one, the passage to manhood and maturity. He was a man of Castile. He was a Spaniard of his time. Or was he? Was he, rather, not the Spaniard but the anti-Spaniard? Wasn't he the one that went against the grain? Superficially, indeed, he seemed very different from the young Castilians all around him. They were so much attracted to the light, and to noise, and he to the dark, and to quietness.

He would not share what Aléjo Venegas described at the time as the Spanish vices. The first was extravagant expenditure on appearances. Juan's poverty kept him in the humblest of garbs. This was, in any case, his dress of choice, with his shrinking from vanity and his preference for unobtrusiveness. So he was an odd man out among the town youths who looked upon their appearance in silken finery as an art. Every one of them was at heart a swaggering grandee whose last economy would be in outward show. And there were many opportunities for them to show their genius for popular display – the fiesta, the bull-fight, even the religious ceremony. This last Juan commented on. 'Too often people make a festival for themselves rather than for God...the ceremony of indiscreet devotion...the more reliance they place on these ceremonies, the less confidence they have in God'. He didn't think the candles, the bells, the incense and the glorious vestments counted for much. To the first, great, specifically Spanish vice, love of surface show, he was foreign.

And Juan sought work, while all around young townsmen shunned it. He had failed in his apprenticeships, in carpentry, in woodcarving, in painting and decorating, in tailoring. So he redirected his efforts into plainer channels, simply carrying out the messy fundamentals in the shadows, in the service of those most in need of them. Most of his fellows looked down on manual work of any kind. To have to work they regarded as a curse upon a man, or at best a misfortune. Wealth should come to a man as his just deserts through the conduit that everyone believed in – suerte. Suerte was the luck, the good luck, the fortune, that rewarded a man for being an exemplary homo hispanicus. The role model was the ubiquitous, idle hidalgo.

Four hundred years later V S Pritchett, in 'The Spanish Temper', found that, 'there is more regard for suerte than for the tedious rewards of industry'. Juan, on the other hand, worked with his hands, and didn't even get paid for it. So, to the second, great, specifically Spanish vice, considering work a default, Juan was, again, foreign.

The third universal vice, mania for ancestral lineage, was closed to the little converso in this time of the statutes of limpieza de sangre and of prejudice. The stain of his 'otherness' would always exclude Juan from his neighbours' notion of the Castilian honour intrinsic to being 'an Old Christian of pure blood'.

The fourth specifically Spanish vice was that of ignorant scorn for learning. And, of course, in no way did Juan share this, the college boy who sat up at his books all night in the woodshed.

More lively nocturnal pursuits were typical of his age group. Matters of sexual behaviour were of great interest. Arguments would rage as to whether fornication really was or was not a sin if a man went only with a prostitute or a low-living, single woman. And there were a lot of such women in Medina del Campo, where more than 80% of the adult poor were female. At times, more than 60% of infants baptised were illegitimate.

But there was one over-arching Spanish passion, the Spaniard's natural passion, and that was pride – pride in his machismo, pride in his specifically Spanish vices, pride in his honour and pride in being prepared to defend that honour as he would defend his life. None of this sat comfortably with Juan who would recommend 'A kind of practice that teaches us to restrain the lust of the flesh, the desire of the eyes, and the pride of life, which are the things that reign in the world and from which all the other desires proceed'.

So, superficially at least, Juan might appear to have been the anti-Spaniard archetype, the negation of idle and showy pride. But there were two sides to the Spanish soul – it might be sol on the outside but it was sombre within. That hidden side, sombre, was where darkness welled up silently into the Spanish consciousness. For all their posturing under the bright sun, Juan's fellows, like Spaniards through the ages, knew that the supreme dignity of man, of Spanish man, was not in his pursuit of style but in his tragic sense of existence. Here Juan joined them in their Spanish identity. (Brenan, 'The Face of Spain')

Behind the facade, the Spaniard had an acceptance of pain and poverty. In the absence of suerte, the perfect Castilian claimed no dues. More than that, he needed nobody. If there was no suerte, there was no shame in poverty and there could at least be gravity and reserve. Castilians respected this and still do. This was Juan too.

Spaniards feed on an inner store of melancholy, thus the importance to them of preserving, then as now, an interior solitude. The Castilian, if alone, can still sit for hours with the mind's engine shut off, a wonderful gift of immobility, of nothingness. This was Juan's nada, nothing, the soul in quietness. 'All must learn to abide attentively and wait lovingly in a state of quiet, and to devote no attention either to imagination or to its working'. 'The soul must remain barren, in total forgetfulness and suspension'. 'The soul journeys, so to speak, by night, in darkness'. 'The soul must proceed by unknowing rather than knowing'.

This was the all or nothing, the todo o nada, the Castilian unadulterated by compromise and pragmatism. Most Spaniards admired the brave ideal of a man staking his whole life to win all, be it repute, honour or his soul.

(Bennassar, 'L'Homme Espagnol'). Few put it into practice, but Juan did. A Castilian paradigm that Brenan describes vividly in 'The Face of Spain'.

For Juan had duende. All Spaniards will talk about the importance of duende, not least Lorca, but it is untranslatable. The dictionary suggests a goblin or an imp. Or magic. More useful is the vague word spirit. But it is always a spirit that lives in the dark. In Castile, between the hardness of the sky and the hardness of the earth, duende can awaken a deep and sombre tremor in a man's blood.

In his lecture, 'El juego y teoría de duende', Lorca described moments of duende yielding themselves in the arts, in music, dance or poetry, in the dark resonances of a performance, in its black sonorities, never repeatable. A glimpse, a note, of duende arouses in the audience the sincere cry of, 'Viva Dios!' This is the human, tender cry of contact with the hidden sacred. 'God is dark night to the soul,' cried Juan in his struggle. Duende's darkness is both tragic and triumphant.

For duende is both a gift and a struggle. Unlike a gift from a muse or an angel, duende wounds. But it is a wound that makes it easier for you to love and die. Man's life's work is to live with the wound. On any man's road towards fulfilment the struggle with his duende awaits him.

Lorca said that Juan's duende made him groan and beat his wings, and only for a moment to take flight with it, at the call to him of his beloved, Christ, the call which appears in his Spiritual Canticle as:

| | |
|---|---|
| Vuélvete, paloma, | My dove turn around, |
| Que el ciervo vulnerado | For the stag they would smite |
| Por el otero asoma | Appears on the high ground, |
| Al aire de tu vuelo, y fresco toma | Refreshed in the air of your flight |

Duende in the original Spanish. Perhaps lost in translation.

Duende is a doubleness – the man and something else, the work and something else, the performance and something else, something dark, something fleeting. Double vision, or double sensibility. In this it is an essence of Spanishness, and it was an essence of Juan.

Beside the parish church of Santiago I go looking for the Colegio Jesuitico where Juan became the man that he was, the Spaniard and the anti-

Spaniard all in one, in one tiny, Castilian frame just four feet ten inches tall. I find no colegio here, of course. College, Jesuits and students have vanished into one great hole in the ground. There is plastic ribbon to stop me falling in with them. There are cement hoppers and cranes, gravel heaps, rutted mud and pools of water. There is a hut labelled 'Informacion y Venta'. Something is for sale here.

Juan moved on. What was he to do with his life? First he went back to work full-time in the Hospital de Bubas. It would never lack for patients. Bubas were endemic. The administrators were delighted and tried to secure him permanently. They offered him the post of chaplain to the hospital, recommending his immediate ordination to the priesthood. Juan did not commit himself yet. He waited and paid loving attention to God. It seemed to him that he was being called to the contemplative rather than to the active life, to be one who served God first rather than man first.

Where would he find this? Where should he look for it? There were several monasteries in Medina del Campo. Right next to the hospital were the Augustinian friars. Juan chose the Carmelites, across town. It seems that certain Carmelite friars had been in contact with him and invited him to join them. Were they voicing God's call? It was on Mount Carmel that Elijah listened for the still, small voice of God and this must have struck a chord with Juan. And then also Mary's presence pervaded the entire Carmelite family, as a model of self-denial, of the contemplative life, the lady to whom they owed allegiance, the elder sister who shared their life, their mother and queen. Juan's own mother, Catalina, and his sister-in-law, Ana, had provided him with just such an exemplary, virtuous, Christian model. In the muddy pond at Fontiveros a beautiful lady had reached out a hand to him, and again, in the well in Medina del Campo, it had been Mary herself. Now he would respond to her.

One day, or as some say, one dark night, without warning anyone, Juan simply walked out of the hospital and down a few streets to the south-west edge of town. Here, just inside the walls, was the still only temporary Carmelite monastery of Santa Ana. He knocked and was taken in.

It was a very small community. He was only the sixth novice to join it. His head was shaved with the monastic tonsure. He was clothed in the dark-brown Carmelite habit and the long white cloak, with its hood. He would wear it for the rest of his life. And he took the name Fray Juan de Santo Matía.

Juan spent his days attending Mass and praying for long hours. He was also able to join classes on grammar and the arts, which were held in the monastery. It was said that he also regularly chose to carry out the very lowliest, menial services in this household of brothers. This sounds consistent. You could take Juan out of the lazaret but you couldn't take the lazaret out of Juan.

After about a year in the monastery, the novice Juan made his profession, received his vows, and publicly entered into the Carmelite Order as a fully-fledged friar. Perhaps Catalina, Francisco and Ana were in the chapel of Santa Ana when this took place.

The chapel was small and the friars lived in a modest house attached to the side of it, rather than in a proper monastic building. I walk to the south-west edge of the old town, barely three hundred yards from the Plaza Mayor, and twice that from Catalina's little house, in search of Juan's first monastery. It had been just by the city walls.

There is still a chapel on the site of Santa Ana. It is built of ancient narrow bricks, and has barred windows and a locked grill across its double doors. A municipal notice beside the door says that this is the chapel of St John of the Cross, San Juan de la Cruz, and that it is permanently closed.

The building next door is an extension of the chapel, in the same good old bricks. It now bears a large plastic sign of the two hieroglyphs that indicate the male and female genders, one interlocking with the other. It seems to house some sort of club where men and women can interlock one with the other. Over the door is an illuminated word, 'Pille'. The adjective, 'pillo,' means wicked. 'Pille' is the imperative of the verb, 'pillar,' which means to catch to get, to nab, as in the English word, pillage. So Juan's first monastery seems to have been converted into a pick-up joint. 'Score'.

The bawdy-house and the iron barred monastic chapel, two sides of Spanishness bound to each other by ancient bricks and mortar in Spanish doubleness.

In late 1564, the twenty-two-year old Juan walked away from this place and headed out of town towards the south-west and Salamanca university. Today the railway line cuts across the meseta, more or less in a straight line and flat, nearly ninety kilometres from Medina del Campo to Salamanca. It goes through nowhere of consequence. In fact it goes through almost nowhere at all. Only very small roads chase it, 'decrepit towns, roads without inns' all the way.

I follow Juan towards Salamanca and, because it suits me to walk on roads with inns, I hope that he took not the shortest but the best road, the road I would like to take. It goes five leagues roughly southward to sleepy old Madrigal de las Altas Torres, and then, bending towards the south-west, another five leagues to the small town of Peñaranda de Bracamonte. Bracamonte is a family name. Peñaranda means a pawnshop.

Four kilometres from Peñaranda, a little, toothless old woman with a red and white dish cloth flapping on her head emerges from an endless, dry field and pauses to put on a day-glo yellow safety waistcoat for the road. She is towing an empty plastic shopping basket on wheels. Later, in town, I see her filling it from municipal rubbish bins.

The convent of the Madras Carmelitas, Carmelite Mothers, in Peñaranda has a small museum. A very old couple show me round. There is a small statuette of Juan and some dark oil paintings. When I pay the old man I see that that euros in his purse are all mixed up with ancient coins with holes in the middle. Not legal tender, at the moment.

The newspaper says that on the northern edge of the meseta vultures have started to kill healthy young cattle rather than waiting for them to grow old and die. Que no quiero verla! How I do not wish to see it! And a wolf has been killing sheep.

Seven and a half leagues to the west, I walk the long, stone, Roman bridge of many arches to cross the river Tormes into Salamanca, a city set upon a hill before me. Cuckoos are calling. Guarding the end of the bridge is another pre-historic stone bull. It is of the same breed as the toros de Guisando. It stands high, now, on a made-to-measure, concrete plinth, as if standing on top of a bus shelter.

# 5 STUDENT OF SOUL IN SALAMANCA

When Juan walked in across the Roman bridge there were no cuckoos calling, for it was December and Salamanca rises out of the plain at nearly 3,000 feet above sea level. Even the honeyed stone of the city may have looked dull under the mid-winter sky. Perhaps he paused by the tawny carved lump that is the ancient bull to consider the romanesque cathedral on the rising ground above him. It was already dwarfed by the scaffolding and the ascending walls of the new cathedral being constructed behind it.

Salamanca was a city of more than 7,000 students from all over the Iberian peninsular and beyond. Its only life was centred on the university, the oldest in Spain. Between the cathedrals, the university and the Plaza Mayor there was a constant buzz, a coming and going of young men in their coloured cloaks of the different colleges and their square black student caps. Among them were the minority in the various religious habits, bareheaded, with shaven tonsures. The regime throughout was of strict discipline and spasmodic rowdiness. This was a brilliant and animated centre of learning that ranked with Paris and Oxford. It was a lovely place and still is. The son of the widowed weaver had come a long way.

Most students entered the university at the age of eighteen. Their aim was to leave it with the reward, the premio, of an assured career as a letrado, a lettered man, in a lay or clerical profession. University was the stepping stone to a good job. Even so, nearly half would drop out before the end of their second year, having run out of funds or intellectual energy.

Juan was older, he was already twenty two. What was the premio he sought? Surely just more understanding of his relationship with God and a more acute ability to put his faith in God to good service. His precise objective was to acquire an exact consciousness of contemplation. 'Contemplation is the science of love'. To the struggle with his dark duende he brought some Carmelite principles: solitude, prayer and meditation, poverty, fasting, abstinence, constant work, silence. He was to be a serious student, in fact an extreme case of serious study.

First he must report to his college. And then he would be entered, or matriculated, on the university register. His matriculation, along with nine other Carmelites from his college, took place on the feast of the Epiphany, January 6th 1565. He was listed under the name of Fray Juan de Santo Matía, a native of Medina del Campo rather than of Fontiveros. It was quite likely that he did not have to be present in person at the matriculation, and that one representative of his college simply entered all ten of them. At some stage during his first year in Salamanca he did have to be present and swear the oath, in front of the Rector, to observe the university's statutes.

Juan was to spend four years as a student in Salamanca. For the first three years he would be an arts student, and would continue, in a more profound and elaborate way, the studies he had pursued at the excellent Colegio Jesuitico in Medina del Campo. At the end of these three years he could move on, all being well, to study theology in his fourth and final year.

The university was centred on several large, lay colleges, each with hundreds of students. Around the fringes of this core were some twenty smaller colleges, each attached to its own religious order. Juan's little Carmelite college was called after San Andrés.

The students who were in religious orders had to attend lectures both in their own colleges and in the central escuelas, the schools of the university. Juan's fellows in San Andrés found his arrival something of a mixed blessing. He was clearly remarkable for his application and for what one of them referred to as his 'outstanding genius'. His virtue became proverbial. In himself he followed an observance of the strictest austerity. But his address to others, albeit limited to academic and religious matters, was helpful and cheerful.

However, living hugger mugger with such a paragon was difficult for the others. Soon he was appointed to a leadership role in the college. He became Preceptor of Studies. His role was to administer in-college teaching sessions and to hear the others in their dissertations and recitations. So now he wasn't just setting, by example, unmatchable standards, but he was also correcting those who fell short of the demands of the order. 'Let's be off – that devil's coming', was sometimes the response to a glimpse of Juan approaching in all goodwill.

And Juan was making life terribly uncomfortable for himself, too. It didn't bother him if the college lived up to a reputation it seemed to have for being a little unwelcoming to new students. He didn't think that he merited anything better. The cell allotted to him was not only dark and narrow but its tiny window actually looked inwards into the gloom of the chancel, the sanctuary. He found it ideal for his purposes, long hours of study by day, long hours of prayer by night. He could remain totally focussed in his cell regardless of the larking about around the place that was sometimes enjoyed by the others. When he ventured out it was a case of, 'Look out, Fray Juan is coming'. It was not that they felt that they were too bad, it was just that having such virtue around can make a normal person feel vaguely guilty. They knew his cell was a miserable slit of shadow furnished only with a work-table, a wooden trough to sleep in, without a mattress and with a block of wood for a pillow. The only book that ever stayed in there with him, night and day, was his Bible.

This would have been a hard, cold way to live had Juan wrapped himself only in his habit and cloak. He chose instead to wear a hair shirt that so scratched his skin that it bled. And sometimes, even worse, to study in his cell in a sort tunic made of knotted strands of rushes common in Spain, esparto grass. He managed to obtain a pair of breeches made of the same harsh material. In Salamanca there must have been mens' outfitters specialising in such painful garments. Unless he somehow plaited, knotted and stitched this strange material together himself. He had, of course, been apprenticed to a tailor for a short while in Medina.

Later Juan would come to see this degree of mortification of the flesh as youthful over-enthusiasm. But now what he was working out for himself was what he would call 'the night of the senses'. Any experience felt through any of his senses must become unpleasant, undesirable. The senses must be cauterised of pleasure. In that way the soul would be stripped of all desires. Only God would be left for the soul. 'For the soul to come to unite itself perfectly with God through love and will, it must first be free from all desires of the will, however slight'.

So Juan wrote the following list of advice so that the soul could enter 'the night of the senses', get rid of its unruly desires for the things of this world and clear the way to God. It can be found in his 'Ascent of Mount Carmel'.

Strive always to prefer not what is easiest,
but what is most difficult.
Not what is most delectable, but what
is most unpleasant.
Not what gives the most pleasure, but what
gives the least.
Not what is restful, but what is wearisome.

And so on. Juan believed that, although achieving 'The night of the senses' is a sore and sorry path, if it is successfully followed through the darkness it will be found to lead to joy and peace, a great light.

In order to arrive at having pleasure in everything,
desire to have pleasure in nothing.
In order to arrive at possessing everything, desire to
possess nothing.
In order to arrive at being everything, desire to be
nothing.
In order to arrive at knowing everything, desire
to know nothing.

This was Juan's nada. Nothing. In nada is to be found todo. Everything. With this last, somewhat contemporary, set of instructions in mind, I go looking for Juan's little Colegio de San Andrés.

Of course, not a trace of it is there. Nada. Just like the house of his birth in Fontiveros, his home in the little square in Arévalo, his home in Medina, his first school, the Hospital de Bubas, the Colegio Jesuitico and the monastery building of Santa Ana, it is gone. Juan has been bulldozed away again. Hid from sight.

I start in the University shop. I ask the lady managing it whether she stocks any books about Juan. 'No, we have no records of him here but we have books on St Teresa. To find out about Juan de la Cruz you must go to Ávila'. Ávila, of course, is Teresa's home town and not Juan's. The shop is full of expensive souvenirs featuring don Quixote, who, even as a fictional character, never came anywhere near Salamanca.

I know that the Colegio de San Andrés was not far from the Roman bridge, so I go down to the river. Some five hundred yards east of the bridge, in a quiet corner, I find a curious statue of my man. He is leaning forward over a desk, holding a quill pen and writing with it without looking at what he is doing. He has been extended from his four foot ten inches to become a lanky, affected, el Greco type figure, well over six feet tall. Again, it's as if this elongated statue is a decoy designed to take one's eye off the real man.

The statue is at the bottom of a small street now called Arroyo de Santo Domingo. In Juan's time it probably was just a real arroyo, a stream or gutter which helped drain the city and flowed out under the walls. This section of the walls has been removed now, together with a gate, the Puerta de San Pablo. Juan's little college was probably just outside the walls where the drain ran out to soak away towards the river.

There is a fine art gallery nearby with a garden, and I convince myself that it has usurped the site of the college. I go in and tell the girl who is supervising the exhibition. She refers me to an armed security guard. He is not sure about it but will ask his colleague when he comes on duty.

I wander out and look at the locked church next door, the church of the Carmen de Abajo, the lower garden. High up on the wall there is a small plaque which says, 'On this site, the old Convent of San Andrés of the Carmelites, lived and studied (1564-1568) St John of the Cross, Doctor of the Church'. This is the place.

I go back and tell the girl at the art gallery and the security guard.

Coming out of his college to head for the university Juan could look up at the cathedrals, old and new. My line of sight is blocked by a modern hotel.

When he left his cell, Juan could never be alone. All meals were taken together in the college. Conversation was not allowed but neither was silence. A reader slowly intoned passages from the Bible or other books of devotion. After the meal there would be an academic debate about what had been heard.

Students were allowed to leave the college only to go to classes and they had to go in pairs, not alone or in groups. The two of them must be wearing their white hooded cloaks over their brown habits and they must walk with religious gravity. It was the custom to go hand in hand. Those who broke the rules were shut in their cells for eight days. If they offended again, it was bread and water for a day and three penitential flagellations with a scourge. The third time the fault was repeated it meant expulsion from the college and a long walk back to the monastery that had sent them to university. There would be more disciplines there. Juan can't have been much fun to pair up with but at least his partner wouldn't have run much risk of incurring punishment.

The first class of the day, at eight o'clock in the morning in winter, seven in summer, lasted one and a half hours, all the rest one hour. The professor gave his lecture in Latin, without reading or referring to notes, and he was not allowed to treat it as dictation. At the end, he was allowed to repeat his conclusion several times, to make it easier for the students to note it down. Some kind professors did actually lecture very slowly so that the students could copy much of it. Some bold students hissed loudly when professors spoke fast. After lectures, the students of the Colegio de San Andrés were expected to pair up again and return with religious gravity, directly to the college. And, once there, Juan did not linger about, chatting, but went up to his narrow cell to study his notes of what he had heard in class. At this stage of his mortal existence he very much kept himself to himself and to God. Life here, so enclosed and constrained, was very different from the open life of his teenage years, hurrying about the streets of Medina from his patients in the Hospital de Bubas to his school-mates in the Colegio Jesuitico to his family in their little house, weaving.

I follow Juan from his vanished college up towards his university classrooms. We pass the bottom of the arroyo, the open drain that has become a narrow street, and we turn through the vanished walls at the vanished gate of San Pablo. The sunny street, the Calle de San Pablo, rises ahead, concretely. A few small shops, bars and restaurants have materialised to cater for today's students where Juan and his fellows had no use for them.

Half-way up, I turn left across the open space on the north side of the new cathedral. A wedding party emerges. Some of the men are wearing tail-coated morning suits like tanned and affluent young Englishmen. The girls are in brightly coloured, flounced skirts. Cigarettes, mobile 'phones and dark glasses are quickly brought into play.

On I go to the Escuelas Menores, the lesser schools, where Juan attended the lectures of the Faculty of Arts during his first three years in Salamanca. I enter a plain courtyard. There are two arches and about fifty regularly spaced windows on three floors. This is as far as I can go, so I turn and make my way down narrow, ancient streets to the Plaza Mayor.

It is the focal point of this lovely city. Since Juan's time it has been rebuilt in colonnaded baroque style to become the most beautiful great square in the finest university town in Spain. Not that Juan would have been able to spend time in it even if it had already been beautiful then.

There are musicians here. There is an acrobat. Small boys kick footballs. Older ladies walk small dogs. Families keep an eye out to pounce on any stone bench that may become available. I sit hip and thigh with ice-cream eaters. Groups of young people, today's Salamanca students, sit on the paving stones in circles of affection. At this time on a bright summer's evening, every evening, Juan sat alone in his dark cell seeking his nada, his nothing, his 'night of the senses'.

At the end of three years of this dedicated concentration, Juan underwent an examination. He presented and defended a thesis against the attacks of the professors of the Faculty of Theology, the faculty he was trying to graduate into from the Faculty of Arts. The event was held in public and the other candidates were allowed to join in with criticisms of his thesis. He passed and in late 1567, aged 25, he became a student in theology, for his final academic year in Salamanca.

Now his lectures were in the main university building, the Escuelas Mayores. The same practices were followed as in the Escuelas Menores, across the street: Latin language, no reading from notes by professors, no dictation, hissing students. The lecture halls were larger and even more crowded. At the end of the hour the professor went out into the courtyard and stood by a pillar, el poste, the post, the students called it. Here they could question him, ask for clarification, make objections (Kagan 'Students and Society in Early Modern Spain')

Juan's most eminent professor was one of the kind ones who spoke slowly and clearly so that student note-taking could keep up. This was Luis de Leon, poet, philosopher, intellectual and friar. That he was translating Solomon's mystical Song of Songs, into Castilian must have made a big impression on Juan, who would later write his own spiritual canticle in Castilian. After Juan left Salamanca, Luis de Leon spent an uncomfortable five-year sabbatical in an Inquisition prison. On his return to his lecture room, he started again with the word, 'Dicebamus...', 'We were saying...' In his lectures to Juan he exalted solitude and the regathering of one's spirit in the fastness of nature. This seed, planted in Juan's cell-bound darkness, would flower in him later, out under the sun and under the stars.

With the influence of Luis de Leon, Juan began to make a special study of mystical writers. This was the year that the young Carmelite friar began to turn away from the path of doctrinal analysis towards the path of spiritual intuition, as a means of approaching mysteries inaccessible to the understanding. It was a critical turning point in his life. The letrado, the lettered man, was turning into a mystic man.

As Hamilton in 'Heresy and Mysticism' and du Boulay in 'Teresa of Avila' record, by the middle of the sixteenth century, mysticism was an epidemic in Spain. Its practitioners were people with no formal organisations or agendas. They were simply taking their own course away from that of the establishment, the letrados. They would be recognised under the title of espirituales, spirituals, or alumbrados, lit up, or illuminati, illuminated. They made the church nervous because the mystic renders the priest and the entire ecclesiastical hierarchy superfluous. In mysticism an immediate knowledge of God is obtained through personal, direct experience. And this in turn sometimes made those mystics over-enthusiastic. They would get carried away and indulge in exaggerated displays of emotion in church or at prayer. Bad form. They increasingly became targets of the Inquisition.

Mysticism appealed to women. And it appealed to conversos, for whom it manifested itself, perhaps, as fresh shoots springing from the severed trunk of an old monotheistic religion. And it seemed to have a particular appeal in the spare lands of Castile. It has been said that mysticism was the true centre of Christianity as conceived by the Castilian (Peers, 'St Teresa of Jesus'). The mysticism latent in the Castilian had an affinity with the nada of the bare meseta, with the dark sonorities of duende and with the doubleness of Castilian vision.

Some alumbrados practised what they called recogiemento.  This meant collecting oneself together, drawing in one's temporal antennae, closing in on oneself so that one was completely disconnected from the world around one, thus leaving the coast clear and oneself tuned in only for God's approach.  Others practised what they called dejamiento.  This was letting go of oneself and of everything, becoming completely passive and open, surrendering to God's approach.  Mystics prayed vocally with the Lord's prayer, they prayed meditationally on the life and passion of Christ, and then, most importantly, they prayed spiritually simply with an empty soul.  It was said that the right size of meal for a mystic was one that enabled him or her to pray after it without falling asleep.

Juan recognised a progression from meditation, which is active, to contemplation, which is passive.  This move required a disengagement of the soul, an emptying of it of all created things, leaving at its centre only its bare essence, where God was found.  God and myself, myself and God, and no world beside. (Peers, 'Spanish Mysticism').

For Juan, mysticism's heartbeat was love for God.  'To leave one's house by the secret, hidden stair, in this night of loving, in this secret on which no-one spied, oh flame of love alive, oh sweetness to be burned!'  The work of mysticism was directed not towards deepening the faith of this believer but towards deepening this believer in his love of God. Love was Juan's life's work.  So all the darkness, the discomfort and the drudgery was well worthwhile.  He was happy with it.

I go looking for the lecture hall where Juan was so influenced by Luis de Leon, a short walk away from the Plaza Mayor, where I have been sitting among the cheerful crowds.  All over Salamanca the ancient bells are ringing out the quarter hours, some reverberant, some cracked, some assertive, some pensive, none synchronised.

The doorway into the university building, the Escuelas Mayores, is set in a stone facade of great beauty, elaborately carved.  Inside there is a courtyard with pillars, the postes where the professors faced their questioners.

Luis de Leon's lecture room seems to be very much in its original state.  The windows are small so the light is not good.  In the centre of the wall facing the door is his raised pulpit with its little, conical roof.  Juan and the others sat at rows of long desks, about sixteen feet long and with their own benches fixed to them. Desk and bench are each made from one solid plank, three inches thick, supported only at the ends. The desk is six inches wide and slightly tilted, the bench five inches wide. They are both hacked out of rough timbers and crudely fashioned, the sort of standard I might achieve if I tried to be a carpenter. I am sure Juan must have left some DNA among these splinters. The basic simplicity is just his style. These desks are not comfortable.

In this very lecture room (Beevor 'The Spanish Civil War'), in 1937, the philosopher Unamuno, Rector of Salamanca university, was shouted down by Franco's gunmen. 'Muera, la inteligencia! Viva La Muerte!' 'Die intelligence! Long live death!' Sacrilege in this place.

My last search in Salamanca for one of Juan's haunts is for the old cathedral, the romanesque one. I manage to get views from different angles of different parts of its fabric but, for some time, I cannot work out how actually to get into it. Eventually I give up and go into the new cathedral instead, which describes itself as gothic style but was built in the early renaissance. It is a tall, impressive place. While Juan was here it was in use for worship only between the west door and the transept, as the east end was still a construction site. Wandering about in the new cathedral, I suddenly find a door in the wall which leads straight into the old cathedral, if you pay at a desk. This is the only way in. It seems to me like restrictive practices. You may go into the old cathedral to worship or sightsee but only if you pay your dues to the new cathedral.

The old cathedral is a magical, shadowy tunnel of golden stone, more intimate than grand. You look through it towards an altarpiece of brighter gold, the finest example of its time outside Italy.

I am sure Juan must have been allowed out of the Colegio San Andrés to come up here sometimes, even if only hand in hand with a reluctant colleague. Wherever he stood for mass, it can't have been more than a few yards from where I stand now.

After passing into the Faculty of Theology Juan was ordained priest. Was it in this perfect cathedral? The last big milestone in its history? The building had already been standing for 400 years. The altarpiece had been up for 100 years. The new cathedral was about to elbow it aside.

So it was time for Juan to return to Medina to say his first mass. It was August: the inferno of the meseta was at its most extreme. Three long days on foot for the young friar and priest, from the Roman bridge back to the little monastery of Santa Ana.

I decide not to walk after him, back to Medina. I shall cut the corner and wait for him to catch up with me on my second visit to the green haven of Duruelo.

As I leave the city I see that a tabloid newspaper headline says, 'Quiero dar mas de mi.' 'I long to give more of myself'. It could be Juan speaking but the newspaper is actually quoting a bullfighter. This is Spain. Todo o nada.

# 6   MAN WITH A MISSION

For ten years, unsparing of himself, Juan had been working day and night, caring for the sick and dying, praying, studying, exercising his mind and his spirit in stern disciplines. What was it all for? Whither now? He would soon have an answer and it would not be the quiet life that he expected.

What Juan expected to do was to settle back into the little Carmelite monastery of Santa Ana in Medina del Campo while preparing to switch to the more contemplative order of Carthusians. With the Carthusians, he could spend the rest of his life in silence in the monastery of El Paular above Segovia in the high, green valley of the Sierra de Guadarrama, beside a clear little babbling river, looking into the darkness while the nightingales sang. But all this was to be blown aside by the cheerful bossiness of Madre Teresa de Jesus.

In the chapel of Santa Ana, Juan said his first mass. His proud family were there, his mother Catalina, his elder brother Francisco, and Francisco's wife Ana. In the monastery beside the church he took up the duties of assistant teacher and planned his move to El Paular.

But a whirlwind was in town. Teresa, like Juan, had the blood of conversos in her veins. She was a woman of great energy, and an extravert. The Madre was fifty two and experiencing a run of success. She was in a hurry. The great Carmelite convent of the Encarnación, outside the walls of her home city of Ávila, had been challenged in its decadence thanks to her righteous example. She had opened a second convent in Ávila, San José, this time under a reformed Carmelite constitution. Now she was opening another one in Medina. Her nuns were to be known as descalzas, unshod or barefoot, symbolising the stark simplicity of their way of life. 'We are called to make a virtue of necessity', said Teresa. Not a bad principle for life, and practical too. As the definitive chronicles of her life I have taken du Boulay's 'St Teresa of Ávila', Peers's 'St Teresa of Jesus' and Bilinkoff's 'The Ávila of St Teresa'.

From an early age Teresa had always shown independence of character. Now she was a middle-aged, strong willed, persuasive manager of women, and of men. As a leader she was down to earth. 'Between the cooking pots walks the Lord,' she said. She loved mirth and gaiety and joy. She had a horror of 'frowning saints'.

When Teresa first met Juan, she felt that 'The Lord seems to be leading him by the hand.' And, 'Small in stature...great in the sight of God'. He was the second Carmelite friar that she recruited into the project of reforming the male Carmelite order and of establishing Carmelite friaries of descalzos. Her first recruit was aged 60, rather elderly for his time. Now she commented, 'We already have a friar and a half to begin the reform of the friars'. Which was the half friar, the old man or the little man?

Teresa herself was of no more than average height and solid rather than slight. She had a big face with long, broad cheeks, a broad forehead and a smallish well shaped chin. Her round, dark eyes, set under big arches, looked determined. She had three beauty spots on her face. Her hands were small and pretty.

The first interview between Teresa and Juan took place in her new convent in Medina. It was in the Calle Santiago near the Palacio de los Dueñas, almost opposite Juan's first school and the church where he had worked in the sacristy. Just down the street was the little house where Catalina, Francisco and Ana lived and worked their looms. Up the street, the other way, was their parish church and, just beyond it, Juan's Colegio Jesuitico. So when he came to meet Teresa for the first time he was, in effect, coming home.

In the course of that first meeting all ideas of retiring into Carthusian contemplation were swept aside. Juan accepted from Teresa the mission of reforming the Carmelite order. They knew it would be a lifetime's task, beset by misrepresentations, misunderstandings, opposition, hostility and hardship. Teresa rejoiced over Juan to her nuns in Medina. 'Our Lord has poured into him great abundance of heavenly wisdom'.

Juan tried on his descalzo garments and showed himself to Teresa and her nuns through the iron grill of their enclosure. No longer would he wear the fine cloth of the Observance, as the unreformed Carmelite order was called. Now his brown habit was of poor frieze, a coarse woollen cloth with nap on one side only. His feet were bare. He was descalzo, unshod.

What was it about, this Carmelite business?  It all began in the First Book of Kings, Chapter 18, 900 years BC.  No less a prophet than Elijah went up to the top of Mount Carmel to pray, 'and he cast himself down upon the earth, and put his face between his knees'.  Carmel means garden and Mount Carmel has always been a green place, a sanctuary, a cool retreat from Israel's harsh fire.  Later Elijah lodged in a cave on Mount Carmel. 'And, behold, the Lord passed by, and a great and strong wind rent the mountains, and brake in pieces the rocks before the Lord; but the      Lord was not in the wind:  and after the wind an earthquake; but the Lord was not in the earthquake:  And after the earthquake a fire; but the Lord was not in the fire: and after the fire a still small voice.  And it was so, when Elijah heard it, that he wrapped his face in his mantle, and went out, and stood in the entering of the cave'.  And there, like Juan, he listened for the word of God.

At some stage in the first millennium after Christ a band of Christian monks settled on Mount Carmel.  Or perhaps, as Jotischky suggests in 'The Carmelites and Antiquity', it wasn't until 1187 when Saladin's capture of Jerusalem drove them out into the wilderness, to live 'by the spring on Mount Carmel'.  Some of them were Frankish, some may have been Orthodox Greeks or Syrians and some perhaps were locals.  They lived apart from each other in nooks and crannies among the rocks and came together in an oratory only to worship.  They were anchorites, religious recluses, hermits, solitaries, ascetics.

Around 1200AD the Carmelite Order was formalised by a constitution, a rule that comprised 16 articles, which was given to the hermits by Albert, the Latin Patriarch of Jerusalem and later saint.  They were to observe fasts and a vow of silence and to devote themselves to prayer and meditation. But, above all, the rule was overwhelmingly concerned with the love of God.  Around 1240 they were driven off the mount by violent saracens. Some were killed.  Others escaped to Cyprus.  Some migrated onwards to Sicily, France and eventually England, where they took root most firmly.

The first chapter of the Carmelite Order was held in 1247 in Aylesford on the Medway, and the rule was eased, the first step towards the comfort that Teresa's reform would eventually challenge.  Now, rather than being solitary recluses providing for themselves, they would be allowed to wander about engaging with people, asking for alms, and congregating in monasteries and convents for mutual support.  In England they would be known by their white cloaks as White Friars.

For 200 years they attracted recruits all over Europe.  The more of them gathered together, the more lax their lifestyle became.  In 1432 the pope legitimised this by giving them a still milder rule than before.  This was the slippery slope that Teresa rejected.  Her reform would hark back to 'St Albert's rule' with its emphasis on poverty, fasting and prayer.

In Calle Santiago, the mission Juan accepted so readily from Teresa was to live by and teach the pure Carmelite precepts.  Union with God is possible and it is the ultimate goal of Carmelite life.  The only possible union with God is in conforming our will with His.  We can conform our will with God's through loving as God does.  To love God, we must love man too as He does.  Perfection for St Teresa consisted in the love of God and the love of our neighbour.  Loving attention to the mystery that is God was already Juan's daily bread.  Now Teresa wanted him to go out and share it, to put love into a world riven by heresies, hatreds and strife.  Juan, after four years buried in his shadowy college cell, agonising in his shroud of knotted grasses, came out from his mortification to engage with life again.

And so off he went barefoot to set up the first reformed Carmelite house for descalzo friars.  It was, of course, in that green haven from the burnt, late summer meseta, Duruelo.  With him went some things that had been collected together for the new monastery – vessels for the church, domestic equipment for the house, holy pictures, five hour-glasses to regulate monastic days and nights and a little money.  But first he must visit Ávila, 75 kilometres, 13 leagues south of Medina.  Two days on the road.

Juan carried a letter from Teresa commending him to a gentleman of Ávila, for whatever help or advice he might need.  He stayed in Ávila only long enough to recruit a stone mason.  When they left Ávila the summer was over.  Nine months of invierno, winter, were setting in.  They kept moving and covered the eight leagues in a day.

I approach Duruelo from the other side, the Salamanca side, from the north-west, through Peñaranda de Bracamonte, Pawnshop of the Bracamonte family.  Peñaranda with its Wild West railway tracks skirting the town and its long dusty central square.  All Peñaranda life is in this square, the extended families at café tables, the immaculately suited and polite lone taxi man always leaning against his spotless car, the empty band stand, the dry fountain, the little boys kicking footballs, the poker faced police station.

My way to Duruelo is mercifully free of bulls this time. But on the path I meet a strange figure, wild, emaciated and bearded. His clothes are ragged and his straw hat is torn. He has a weary dog with him. He could pass for Robinson Crusoe but he tells me he is a peregrino, a pilgrim, on his way to Lourdes. He sleeps by the wayside and eats only milk, honey and bread. In towns he begs butchers for meat for his dog. Now he asks me for money 'sin obligación', without obligation, which I happily give him. In Castile one feels close to the past. Closer to the past than to the present sometimes.

# 7   DURUELO – PUTTING UP A GREAT CROSS IN THE DESERT

Before I reach Duruelo myself, I stop one evening in a village to attend mass. It is a dank little church dedicated to Santiago, St James. There are about seventy villagers present. The women are all in the front. The men stand at the back by the double doors, some of them inside, some outside, where it is getting dark. The smell of a dying bonfire seeps in. Thunder rumbles and crackles all around. The dim electric lights flicker on and off. A bat flies around the priest's head. There doesn't seem to be much praying or devotion going on. Just to be present is enough, inside or out.

In 'South from Granada', Brenan described just such a village scene in the 1920s. 'Other men stood outside the church and considered that they had heard mass if they merely looked through the door and crossed themselves when they heard the bell for the elevation. Dogs ran in and out…there was a general atmosphere of indifference'. He went on to say that his researches showed that it was just like this back in Juan's time.

It suggests superstition rather than religion. It suggests going through the motions, like touching wood and throwing a pinch of salt over one's left shoulder. It was important to go through the motions to ward off storms, droughts, diseases and other threats to persons, to livestock and to crops. Religious observance was very much associated with fertility. It had its place in a whole pantheon of taboos and superstitious beliefs. Images were important and were genuflected and bowed to, caressed and carried around ritually on important days.

Juan was quite clear what he thought of all this. He would write in his 'Ascent of Mount Carmel' that, 'We may say of them they were making a festival for themselves rather than for God'. He also said that, although churches are pleasant places furnished for prayer, it is better to choose a solitary place, the most free from distractions, for a matter as intimate as conversing with God. 'Let these people know that the more reliance they place on ceremonies the less confidence they have in God'. As for images, he said that many people displayed great stupidity towards them, setting great store by them, whereas the soul should immediately raise up its mind from the image to what it represents and should centre its sweetness, its rejoicing and its devotion on that.

In moving away from the educated, urban level of the religion of the universal church, and setting himself down in the wilderness, Juan was encountering the religion of place for the first time. Each village would have its own cult. A newly arrived village priest would have to learn that the cult was deeply embedded in the home landscape and transcended the doctrinal abstractions he had learnt in the seminary. For this reason, newly ordained priests were often sent back to be pastors in the countryside of their origin, usually one priest for fewer than fifty families. Rawlings in 'Church, Religion and Society in Early Modern Spain' and Christian in 'Local Religion in Sixteenth Century Spain' have catalogued and chronicled the peculiarities.

Every village had its own traditions and ceremonies, its own images and relics. Always there were obscure shrines and often unofficial local saints. The saints could intercede for the individual as they stood closer to God. The practice of religion was intrinsically interwoven with patterns of work and leisure, the church frequently a setting for local social and commercial activities, village assemblies, singing, dancing, even games.

To strengthen their defences against plague, locusts, lightning strikes and so on, people would often not only go through the motions at mass but also make specific, personal vows. It could be a vow to give money, or to make special acts of devotion, or to go on a pilgrimage. One person might promise charity, another chastity. Sometimes a repeated act became a habit with the original purpose of the vow forgotten, except that it was to do with life and death, of course. Heaven, hell and purgatory were places as real to these people as distant Madrid, Lisbon and Granada.

Heaven and hell, saints and sinners, bells, books and candles, the parish priest besides being the spiritual intermediary for all this was often the temporal agent who performed the role of public notary, sanctioning not just births, deaths and marriages but also contracts, leases, wills and so on. At a price. Right through Juan's lifetime the wealth of the Spanish church never stopped increasing. The head of the church in Spain, the Archbishop of Toledo on his throne was, after the King, the richest man in Spain. While everywhere the common people walked the earth making the sign of the cross. 'Let it be what God wishes,' 'If God wills it,' 'God protect you,' 'Go with God'.

This was the Christian tradition, little changed today at the local level, into which Juan came hurrying then, with his life half spent on preparation already, to make a difference with his message of love.

When Juan and the stone mason arrived in Duruelo on the first evening, footsore, from Ávila, they found that the small farmhouse that a gentleman had donated to Teresa for the first monastery of descalzo friars was just a dirty shack. Teresa had warned Juan, but he had assured her that it would be to his liking even if it were a pigsty.

And so it was to his liking. It was very small and shoddily built. There was an incongruous porch and then a main room, a smaller room which was perhaps just a closet, and a tiny kitchen. Somehow an upstairs fitted in like an overgrown shelf. The main room was to be the chapel of the monastery. The upstairs shelf arrangement was to become the choir. The closet was to be divided into two small sleeping cells which had to be crawled into. The pillows were of stone, the bedding of hay. The kitchen would be the refectory.

After the long walk, Juan and the stone mason ate what food they carried with them and lay down to sleep on the ground. First thing next morning, they set to work, Juan still barefoot, the first pioneering descalzo since the Carmelites had been driven off Mount Carmel, and wearing the rough habit of the Reform. Juan assisted the hard-working mason as a bricklayer's labourer. All day they worked without a break. And the next day and the next. The peasants of Duruelo were amazed to find that an intense little building site had burst into action in their midst. At nightfall they brought bread to these builders. Juan commented that they were better satisfied with this 'than with pheasants', of all strange comparisons. Nearby was the pure flow of the spring that still waters this green haven in the meseta for the very occasional traveller like me.

Soon there were two other friars with Juan. And the enthusiastic stonemason announced that he wanted to become a lay brother in this brand new Carmelite Reformation. Juan's 38-year-old brother, the kindly weaver Francisco, also turned up from Medina del Campo to become the priory's general handyman for odd jobs and dirty work. Not far behind came Francisco's wife, Ana, to wash and clean and tidy, and the brothers' mother Catalina, to cook. Juan was so happy here, just as the cheerful red nosed lady in the rugby shirt promised me. I am happy here for him too.

They put up a great wooden cross in front of the porch, disproportionately large. Juan decorated the inside of the chapel with the holy pictures, unframed, that Teresa had given him for this purpose. The hour glasses were put in place and the days and nights were measured out. They worked 'til dusk and then ate and slept. At midnight they rose to celebrate Matins. After that it was silent prayer until five o'clock when the working day started.

When they stood back and looked at what they had done, they saw that it was good. They were ready for the formal opening of the first reformed Carmelite monastery, a brotherhood of descalzos, the barefoot. When Teresa saw what they had achieved she called it 'A veritable little stable of Bethlehem'. But she was alarmed by the extreme austerity of the way they chose to live. She asked them to modify their rigour a little. She was afraid that they might fall sick and thus enable the devil to hamper their great opportunity for good work. They paid little heed. Later her request turned to an order that, although descalzos, they must put on sandals to journey in the snow and ice. Teresa also warned Juan against always trying to get into a state of total mystical exaltation in order to commune with God. 'It would be a bad business for us if we could not seek God until we were dead to the world...God deliver me from people who are so spiritual that they want to turn everything into perfect contemplation' (du Boulay). With more years, and more experience, Juan himself would be gently passing on this kind of advice against extremism to his own novices and juniors.

On the 28th November 1568, two months after Juan's arrival, the inauguration of the little monastery in Duruelo took place. Six members of the Carmelite hierarchy visited, two of whom would stay on as friars. Juan and his colleagues approached the altar and promised to live in future by the Rule of St Albert, Patriarch of Jerusalem, as it had been formalised, corrected and approved by papal bull in 1247. They were to fast and pray and focus on love as St Albert's primitive rule required of them but, rather than hide away in nooks and crannies as invisible anchorites and hermits, they might move around in the world and gather in monasteries to concentrate their spiritual energies.

Juan, standing beneath the great wooden cross they had put up, took it as his new name. No longer would he be the brother called Fray Juan de Santo Matía. Now he would be, and still is today, Fray Juan de la Cruz.

Juan's days were spent going out into the surrounding countryside and preaching in the villages and hamlets. Some of these might have no priest, others might have a priest content simply to stage the rituals of the masses and the festivals that his parishioners counted on as necessary talismans against hard times and hell. Juan would leave the monastery after the service of Prime at five o'clock in the morning. Sometimes Francisco went with him. They might walk as far as two leagues. When they arrived at a settlement Juan would hear confessions until it was time for mass, which the priest, if there was one, might lead. Juan would give the sermon, teaching of the love of God. Priests and parishioners don't seem to have objected to these missionary incursions. The missionary himself was so little and gentle and his message was one of such humility and love. Duruelo even started to attract visitors. They wanted to absorb some of the energy that this small spiritual powerhouse was generating.

Indeed, Teresa found on her visits that there were people living in the neighbourhood of Duruelo who were receiving the teaching of the friars as if it were welcome rain watering the dried out dust of the meseta. Bread, vegetables and fruit were brought gratefully to the door of the little monastery. The descalzos found that they had more than they needed and distributed some of it to the needy they encountered as they walked and walked from village to village, hamlet to hamlet.

About six months after the inauguration, the Father–Provincial under whose jurisdiction came all Carmelites in the area, whether unreformed calzos or reformed descalzos, turned up in Duruelo and raised the status of the house from a monastery to a priory. This meant that they would be receiving novices. Sure enough, the first two arrived in the autumn and more were on the way. The establishment was becoming too big for its tiny premises. Its days in Duruelo were numbered.

The village of Mancera de Abajo is just over a league away from Duruelo, west along the dusty path where my two bulls lurked. Beyond it the meseta stretches, treeless, to a very far horizon. Unlike Duruelo, Mancera was big enough to merit a palace with its own church. In the palace lived a generous lord of the manor who suddenly offered the descalzos the church and land beside it for a monastery. Within three months the buildings were up and the friars were in, once again with a plea from Teresa for them not to be too hard on themselves, 'for the enemy of goodness is too much' (Lauzeral 'Quand l'amour tisse un destin'). It was June 1570.

I walk the familiar path to Mancera and out onto the road which runs into the village. A great flock of sheep is crossing this road and there is dust in the air. The sheepdog loops menacingly around them towards me, running at the crouch, jaws half open. I pick up a stone, but the shepherd calls him off. I am always frightened of any dog larger than a terrier running at me but I have been advised that I should fear them less in Spain than in France. In Spain, apparently, they learn from an early age that a man with a stick really will give a dog a beating.

I find the church in Mancera de Abajo, but it is not Juan's church. That has completely disappeared, along with its quickly built monastery. Their vegetable garden may still be there, but which is it? There is nobody around to ask. Rather too readily I give up and start to walk back to Duruelo. Even after the move to Mancera Juan often came back this way too to revisit his beloved and abandoned first descalzo priory and to pray there.

In late 1570 one of Teresa's young novices called in at Mancera on her way to join the new convent in Salamanca. She was Ana de Jesús, a beautiful and intelligent young woman. She and Juan made a very good impression on each other, with a particular alertness to each other, which was to endure until Juan's death. They would be able to meet often and spend many hours together in a few years' time. Theirs was a lifelong affair, certainly an 'affaire du coeur', an affair of shared love, an affair in the love of God, an affair of faith.

For nearly two years Juan was much away from Mancera, summoned hither and thither by Teresa to deal with problems and needs arising from the reforming of Carmelite friars. In October 1570 he went to Pastrana, east of Madrid, a journey of some 200 kms, 36 leagues, three or four long days cross-country over rough ground, in order to organise the monastery there along the lines of Mancera. He was back in Mancera within four weeks, luckily in time for the brief visit of Ana de Jesús. In January 1571 it was to Alba de Tormes near Salamanca to help Teresa set up a convent. Juan gave physical help in preparing the building and spiritual help in preparing the nuns. Three months later he was called to Alcalá de Henares, near Madrid, to organise a new university college for descalzo Carmelites. While there he had to pay a second visit to Pastrana to mitigate the excessive fervour of penances and disciplines that some of the young friars were imposing on themselves. Juan was moving towards more moderation. But all this busy hiking about meant that he never set foot again in Mancera nor in his happy Duruelo.

I do not follow Juan here and there on these urgent missions. He was about to be summoned by Teresa to his next major permanent posting, in her home town of Ávila. I set out to catch up with him there, first of all via that long dusty square that makes up the centre of Peñaranda de Bracamonte. There is a funeral passing through it. The taxi man, dark suited, still waiting by his shining car, is smarter than any mourner.

The road to Ávila starts by roughly following the line of the railway. The first two leagues takes in three tiny villages – Cantaracillo, a snatch of song, Gimialcon and Salvadiós, God saves. Here the old route, the one Juan took the first time he came to Duruelo from Ávila, takes a more southerly line but today peters out and vanishes before it gets to Santo Tomé de Zabarcos and on over the heights of Martiherrero, blacksmith's hammer.

The newer road takes the lorries on past the left-turn to Fontiveros, where it all started for Juan, Chaherrero, Muñogrande and into San Pedro del Arroyo, with the only inn on the road, six leagues from Peñaranda and another five to the centre of Ávila. From here the road climbs steadily towards the walled city, while the railway, in an effort to stay on the level, disappears off to the left into a series of twists and tight turns in the bottom of gulleys and gorges.

The road comes in from the west through the city walls, the best preserved medieval city walls in Spain and already 400 years old when Juan came in this way. It is cold. We are more than 3,500 feet above sea level.

In just four years since leaving his dark university cell Juan had found the world, 'thy will be done on earth as it is in heaven', as a preacher, a teacher, a builder, an organiser and a leader. Mostly this was on the move, out under the great sky of the meseta. Now he was called by Teresa to bury himself again, this time in a seething institution in Ávila, a great ant-heap enclosing a regiment of intent and celibate women of all ages.

## 8   JUAN AND THE WOMEN IN ÁVILA

I walk into the centre of Ávila.  The walled city is less than one kilometre long and less than half a kilometre wide.  The intricate medieval street plan has been maintained and another intense burst of maintenance is going on as I pick my way through.  The fabric of the city is in turmoil.  There are cranes, drills, ditches and gravel heaps all over the place.  Fortunately none of this affects the walls which provide a quiet, elevated, uncovered ambulatory, all the way round, half a league, half an hour.  This is the highest provincial capital in Spain and the only completely walled medieval city in Europe.  The walls are pierced by nine gateways and embellished by eighty-eight towers.  They were built, with the help of Moorish masters of geometry and of Moorish prisoners of war, to enclose a city of knights, Ávila de los Caballeros.

One of these caballeros must have later knocked down Juan's first lodging here.  It was in the monastery for calzos Carmelites that Juan, the descalzo, first dwelled in Ávila.  It stood then just inside the north wall of the city, towards the north-east corner.  Noblemen's palaces with their gardens seem to have taken over this stretch of town.  Anyway Juan didn't stay here long.

Soon he moved down to live beside the factory, so to speak.  Teresa had recently taken over as prioress of the unreformed Carmelite convent of the Encarnación and appointed Juan to be confessor to the nuns.  The building was of brick and massive stone, a few hundred yards outside the city, to the north and below it.  Beyond, the ground rises again and then stretches to the horizon with rock and scrub and grass, sheep territory.

Encarnación had been opened in 1515 and, by the time Teresa took over, had had more than 50 years to develop into what has been referred to as ' a Babylon of a monastery' (Lauzeral).  It housed 130 women, most of them from Ávila and the surrounding districts.  Many of them spent long periods out of the monastery visiting families and friends.  Similarly, the three parlours for visitors were always thronged.  Parlours, parley places, talk rooms.  Teresa described the place, in a letter to a friend, as 'pandemonium', a place of all the demons.  Daily life consisted of visits, treats, gossip, fibs, the passing of secret notes, the reading of romances, and singing and dancing together (Peers, 'Handbook to the Life and Times of St Teresa'). But, by the time Juan arrived, things were better. Teresa was able to 'praise the Lord for the change He has wrought in them' and note that 'almost all are improving'.

Teresa promised to these spirits on the mend a much needed and very special confessor: 'I am bringing you, ladies, a saint for confessor'. So, in mid 1572, Juan, aged just 30, moved into his cottage with its own little courtyard right up against the south-west wall of the flowery garden enclosure of Encarnación. On the other side of the wall was a community of 130 women of all ages, still mildly seething but at least improving from their earlier state of agitation, indulgence and laxity. Juan's cottage was called by the nuns the Casa de la Torrecilla – the house of the little tower, the house of their token man.

How did Juan cope? He was a man who had had little adult contact with women and was now surrounded by them, but he perhaps developed a natural sympathy for them more readily than he was able to feel for men of his own age (Brenan, 'St John of the Cross'). Certainly, as the only young man on the premises he must have been a focus of attention and an object of great interest to all those women.

After Juan had been with the women for two years their prioress, Teresa, moved away, back to her little convent of descalzas, San José, some 500 yards to the east of the city, along the ridge which Ávila crowned, leaving Juan to stand alone in the valley below. Before she left an incident occurred in which Juan was said to have levitated. He was talking and praying with Teresa through the iron grille in the wall that separated two little parlours, with their floors of dark red brick, whitewashed walls and ceilings of blackened wood. They were talking of the great mystery of God when suddenly Juan was silent and the next moment appeared to rise up as if by an irresistible impulse. A nun was just entering and later spoke of Juan rising to the ceiling. Shortly afterwards Teresa, with all her down to earth influence, was on her way, leaving Juan more than ever the little hero of Encarnación.

The nuns came to depend on him more and more. When a terrible storm of thunder and lightning broke right upon the convent, they all rushed to the oratory to commend themselves to God under Juan's guidance. And, under his guidance, the house was being transformed and the unruliest of girls becoming souls of quiet interior life.

For love of their confessor, they would sometimes send dainty dishes to his cottage. Always he would send them back into the convent with instructions that they be given to the sick.

For love of her confessor, one girl delivered herself in person to his table. He was sitting eating in his cell with the door open into his yard when suddenly she was there with him. She had climbed over the wall from the enclosed garden of Encarnación. She was a beautiful and well-educated young woman of noble family. He reprimanded her calmly, she apologised and he sent her back with love. As he said to another young nun, he himself was not a confessor who was holy but that the holiness he sought in confession was in gentleness and in not being scandalised at other people's faults, through coming to understand man's weak condition better.

Another attractive young nun was being constantly visited by a rich gentleman of the town, who brought her gifts and turned over to her large sums of money. This was causing worry and discussion both in the convent and in the man's family. The nun began to go to confession with Juan and in a short time decided not to see the man again. The furious gentleman blamed Juan for the girl's change of heart and lay in wait one night outside the church of Encarnación. When Juan came out to walk the few yards to his cottage against the wall the man set upon him and beat him savagely with a cudgel until he lay battered and helpless upon the ground. Neither man referred to the incident again except that once, some time later, Juan said, curiously, that the blows had been as sweet to him as the stones to St Stephen.

At another time one of the older nuns fell seriously ill. Her sisters tried every remedy they could but she continued to fail. Eventually they decided to move her to a better, more comfortable room, but on the way, lying on the mattress on which they were carrying her, she lost consciousness and appeared to have died. They sent for Juan urgently and he was allowed into the enclosure, although it seemed that it was too late and that he had not taken the care to give the dying woman confession and the sacraments in time. Juan looked down at the body for a few moments and then went down into the church to pray for her. After a short while the nuns came rushing to him saying that the dead woman had returned to life again. So he went back up to her and prepared her for a proper death in her own good time. The nuns were convinced that they had witnessed a miracle on the part of their holy confessor. Juan's reply was that for them to make much account of miracles, setting great store by such signs of God's real presence in the world, was to lessen the merit of the blind faith in God they already had without a miracle in sight. It was not God's will to work miracles, he told them.

The next woman problem that Juan was dragged into was a rather more complicated and protracted affair, and it took place in an Augustinian convent on the other side of town, Nuestra Señora de Gracia, just outside the walls, at the south-east corner. There was a nun there who was a prodigy, aged about twenty. She had first come there, to boarding school, at the age of five. By now she was a precocious theologian, explaining the Holy Scriptures brilliantly although she had been taken through no course of studies and had listened to no master. Many people would visit the convent to hear her. Her superiors began to be uneasy. The top scholars from the University of Salamanca, including Juan's teacher Luis de Leon, were called to examine her, one after the other. They found that her spirit was good and her knowledge was wonderful. But the superiors grew still more uneasy. Where did her extraordinary utterances spring from? They sent for the young man who was achieving such great things with the women in Encarnación. Juan was reluctant but at last, with the approval of the Inquisition in Ávila, took up the task.

Juan started a series of visits to the girl in Nuestra Señora de Gracia. He never came alone. One or other friar of Ávila would accompany him each time. Juan would go into the confessional and usually spend about an hour with the girl. At the end of the first session he came out and told the waiting authorities, 'This nun is possessed by the devil'. Consternation. He was commissioned to conduct an exorcism. It would be a tricky undertaking and would have to be closely witnessed and monitored since it was so open to charlatanism. Demonic possession was often related to sexual temptation and sexual exploitation of women by men. Its exorcism often took the form of physical, even intimate, contact between the possessed and the exorcist. Sometimes possession manifested itself only when the exorcist was present. The woman usually believed she had a pact with the devil (Green, 'Inquisition – the Reign of Fear').

The exorcisms in the convent of Nuestra Señora de Gracia lasted several months. Juan used to go up there once or twice a week. The other young nuns in the convent used to react to his visits with great warmth and some came to address him on familiar and affectionate terms. This was not helpful to a man trying to focus on the hard ordeal of exorcism.

The poor girl possessed readily confessed that she had given herself to the devil when she was six years old. She had cut her own arm open and written with her own blood that she was the devil's for ever. During the exorcisms she would go into terrible convulsions, foam at the mouth, howl terrible insults at Juan and have to be restrained from springing upon him. When she was calmer they would argue about verses from St John's gospel, such as 'The Son of God became man and lived with us', which she insisted she read not as 'with us' but 'with you'. She was so committed to the devil that she wept that there should be anyone who loved God. Gradually, over the weeks, through fasting and prayer, the girl slipped out of the clutches of her hysterical heresy and back into the all-enveloping, quiet security of the shared faith that governed all around in her community. Finally she was free of the devil and back in the hands of God.

Thus Juan became even more celebrated among the religious of Ávila. Soon he was called upon to exorcise another possessed nun's demon. Fortunately he accomplished this in just one day. But mending all these damaged, demented, half-dead, and devoted women took a lot out of him. Nightmares and infirmity wore him down. He believed that it was the devils themselves tormenting him.

And his work in Encarnación was so demanding. He was expected to pull his weight in the convent's church, day in day out. Matins took place two or three hours before sunrise. Then there was Lauds, for the singing of psalms. The first daylight service was Prime. Next was Mass, for the celebration of the Lord's Supper with the sacraments of bread and wine. Terce was held at the end of the first third of the day, say ten o'clock in the morning. Sext was at the sixth hour of the day, midday. Nones was not until three hours later, the ninth hour of the day. Vespers was evensong, at about six. Compline was the last, the completing service of the day, at around nine o'clock. And so to bed. And in between times there were the nuns to confess individually, each one at least once a fortnight, up to a dozen a day.

In some ways, Juan could be seen to be working almost as a functionary of the Spanish monarchist state, helping to hold its unique fabric together. The very year that he arrived in Ávila, the king issued a royal decree denying the pope any jurisdiction over the church in Spain (Kamen, 'Spain 1469-1714. A Society of Conflict'). The king now embodied Spanish, religious, national unity, defining and driving the Spanish way of Christianity as a mission to extirpate religious incorrectness and heresy. And the Spanish mind revelled in the painful, self-sacrificing side of its religion (Hume, 'The Spanish People').

What the whole confessional system fuelled was a morality that governed through an internal sense of sin. A guilt culture was created. Confessors were expected to drive the system through the use of shame or fear. And by the middle of the sixteenth century it was, indeed, a system. There were many confessors' manuals published in Castilian and circulated throughout Spain. The manuals were abundant and cheap and it was presumed that the laity would read them, too, as an aid to confession (Homza, 'Religious Authority in the Spanish Renaissance'.)

Confessions typically began with an opening exchange between priest and penitent, and then the Lord's Prayer and Ave Maria before consideration of the penitent's transgressions. There was a shift in emphasis taking place, with the seven deadly sins receiving less attention (ire, intemperance, sloth, pride, avarice, lust, envy), and transgressions against the Ten Commandments taking centre stage. This meant a shift from flexible interpretation to the arbitrary, from relative to absolute. Confessors were supposed to target only the transgressions that were most relevant to the specific penitent and not to resort to aggressive questioning, but many would have derived their understanding of penance from the authoritarian tone of some of the manuals.

Many, no doubt, enjoyed their power over their penitents to pursue detailed enquiries, particularly into their sexuality. Where a young male confessor and a young female penitent were concerned, priest and penitent might come to take great pleasure in each other and in the discussion of sinfulness, and the confession might be strung out for an hour or more (Green, 'Inquisition – the Reign of Fear').

Juan had neither the time nor the inclination for this approach, even though it might have appealed to some of his young nuns. He probably favoured the attributes of a good confession defined in one manual, namely that it should be frequent, voluntary, simple, humble, pure, faithful and clear (Homza).

Juan also worked for the good of his nuns in less formal ways. He would go out into the city and ask for money to improve their lot. He would bring back delicacies for those who were suffering. He would give them the wherewithal for them to provide themselves with the basics, such as a pair of shoes. If they were sad he would spend time talking with them to cheer them up. He would write encouraging maxims and exhortations on pieces of paper and leave them lying about for the nuns to find. It was in Encarnación that he began to put together his collection of Dichos de luz y amor, sayings of light and love. As he led the community towards a greater spirituality, towards where they had not been before, many of them came to adore and venerate him. When asked how he did it, he replied, 'God does it all, and for that he directs me to love them well'.

This was all well and good, all this light and love, but there must have been something of a dark side to it too. For he was a young man mostly incarcerated now within forbidding stone walls, while his previous four years had been spent in the joy of walking and talking, teaching and preaching in the great, natural world of the meseta, under the sun and under the stars. And he was a young man who had walked alone, a free agent but who now found himself entangled in a complex web of women's ways, a web of emotional and rational unpredictabilities, of spiritual and sexual tensions, of love and wickedness, and a web, apparently, just for him.

These may have been the pressures driving him to go deeper into the mystical life that he had discovered at university in Salamanca. He needed to be able to turn away from his urgent stressful harem of Encarnación and seek healing refuge in his beloved nada, nothing, darkness, what he called the dark night of the senses.

The path to the sanctuary of his own Mount Carmel, el camino de la negación, the path of negation, would later be the subject of one of his finest poems, 'En una noche oscura', on a dark night.

He elaborated that mystical path in his prose work, 'Ascent of Mount Carmel'. One must start one's journey by gradually depriving oneself of all desires for worldly things, so that one can travel unencumbered. Desires for worldly things are like restless, discontented children who are always demanding this or that from their mother and are never satisfied. To lose one's worldly desires of the senses is to find one's night of the senses, untroubled quiet and repose.

Thus, one's 'house being now at rest' one may go forth on this dark night to journey towards God, to meet one's Beloved. At this stage of the journey, one's two interior senses of imagination and fancy must be stilled into darkness too. The reason for this is that our imagination and fancy can fashion internal mental constructs only with matter picked up from previous empirical experience. To try to think of constructs of God's mystery using these mundane internal senses is to lead oneself astray in one's approach to God. The mind, the soul, the self must be wiped clean like a blank slate for the mystery that is God to write love on.

So we must all learn to abide attentively and to wait lovingly on God in a state of quiet, with our faculties passive, not active. Juan warned, 'When your mind dwells on anything, you are ceasing to cast yourself on the All'.

He suggested that in order to achieve this state one might need first to go through a period of active meditation on sacred subjects as a means of settling oneself. But what was most important was to learn to be still and passive in metaphorical darkness, simply fixing loving attention on the unfigurable mystery that is God. Thus, he assured us, little by little God's divine calm and peace will be infused into us, enfolding us in love.

Juan acknowledged that we might find this journey into the night of the senses difficult. But he himself had developed the knack. Somehow he managed to seem so often 'unalterably serene as if he had no passions, absolute master of all the impulses of soul and body' (du Boulay).

However, it didn't totally work. Juan could feel great frustration with himself sometimes in failing to reach that place where he could experience union with God. And great frustration with God sometimes not coming to him in that place where he abided lovingly, attentively and passively. So he wrote a poem about his frustration. Perhaps, also, his women added another dimension to the frustration of his situation. He had always to be with them and yet always to be without them.

Juan called this first major poem he attempted, 'Coplas del alma que pena por ver a Dios', verses of the soul that pains to see God. It is rather a wordily contorted complaint, words more of the mind than of the heart and soul. It is a poem of frustration by a winged love poet held grounded and hostage within his intelligence and his profession. It is the least engaging of his poems, and my translation of it is the least engaging of my translations. More significantly, it is simply a remake of a poem written by Teresa a year or two earlier. (Peers, 'The Complete Works of St Teresa of Jesus. Vol III). That one starts with the same line as Juan's, each stanza ends with similar words, and the construction is identical in lines and rhymes. Juan must have been struck by the cleverness of Teresa's composition and decided to produce a version personalised to his own unhappiness.

The first four stanzas insist that living his life in the absence of God is like living in a sort of painful limbo, and in fact living this way is more like being dead, living death, to which real death would be preferable.

> I live not in me,
> And in such-wise on stand-by,
> Of not dying I die.
>
> In me I live not,
> Without God no way;
> As without me I stay,
> To live that is what?
> A thousand deaths got,
> Then my life the same stand-by,
> Of not dying I die.

This living I do
Is life's privation;
And death's continuation
'Til lived with you;
My God hear me true,
This life I deny;
Of not dying I die.

My absence from you,
What can it contain,
But a death-throe of pain,
More than ever I knew?
Pity I hold to,
Stubborn lot I apply,
Of not dying I die.

Next, in comparing himself with a fish hauled ashore which can at least console itself with the knowledge that its death is of value to someone, he regrets that whether he dies or goes on living is of equally no account to himself or anyone else.

The fish out of sea,
Can solace retain,
That death to sustain,
Some value may be;
What in death requites me
Living wounded so sore,
As to live more is to die more?

Then he turns to the idea that going to mass and seeing the sacraments ought to help but that, alas, it makes things even worse for him when he finds he doesn't see in them what he longs for, God.

Thinking to calm me
With seeing your sacrament,
More is my sentiment
Powerless to charm me;
All the more does it harm me,
My beloved not to spy,
Of not dying I die.

And now he thinks that even hoping to see his Lord is aggravating his problem because it makes the fear of not seeing him so much more acute.

> If, Lord, I delight,
> In hoping to see you,
> That I lose you to view
> Redoubles my plight:
> Living in fright,
> Waiting hope I,
> Of not dying I may die

So he asks God for life, to be freed from this living death which he is dying of because he cannot see God.

> From this death extradite,
> Make my life, God, your gift;
> Not held in this shift
> In coils so tight;
> See I pain for your sight,
> My malaise is so total,
> That not dying is mortal.

Finally he decides that in his current predicament, the result of his own sins, he must equally mourn both his own life and his own death. He asks God when at last he may be able to say truthfully that he is alive (in this life or the next, of course) and no more caught up in the process of dying.

> Weep shall I death then,
> And life me lament
> In as much its internment
> For my sins did happen.
> Oh my God! To be when?
> To say when and believe:
> Of not dying I live?

Somewhat oppressed by this gloomy meditation, I take another walk around the walls of Ávila. Juan's faith, so intense that it could be a form of acute suffering, makes me feel like a shallow, easy-going, lightweight sort of fellow traveller. Half-hearted. Perhaps taking to the discomfort of the road again will give my search a bit more depth.

At the south-east corner of the city walls I look out and down onto the convent of Nuestra Señora de la Gracia. In earlier days there had been a mosque on this site, and then later a Christian shrine. Later still the Augustinian convent to which Teresa came as a schoolgirl to board. By the time Juan arrived to carry out his exorcism the place was steeped in religious history. What I see now is the enlarged and improved building.

Around the convent are clustered some buildings of the modern age and then a fair, green plain. I can follow with my eye the road across it along which I am going to track Juan southwards, into the mountains beyond, and on to Toledo.

I climb down from the walls, go out through the gate of the Alcázar and come to the studded wooden door of the convent. I can go no further. I listen to the silence of many nuns. Just as, it is said, in London you are never more than 15 feet away from an unseen rat so, in Ávila I feel, you are never more than 5 metres away from an unseen nun.

I head through the city to make my visit to Encarnación and, on the way, I come across a pleasant bronze statue of Juan, life-sized and a good likeness. He is in a hurry, walking fast by the look of it, hands together holding a small cross, face tilted slightly upwards.

I come down towards Encarnación from the city walls through several hundred yards of very neat, quite attractive, small suburban villas. I can see that they don't stretch far beyond the convent before giving way to a timeless, scrubby terrain, the swell of which subsides into the flatness of the far meseta.

Once inside Encarnación, I am allowed into only three rooms. I am taken into the little parlour and shown the iron grille in the wall through which Juan used to talk to Teresa and where he once appeared to levitate. I am allowed into the church and watched as I snoop around it. It has been much transformed into a chapel dedicated to the sainthood of Teresa.

I am then locked into the museum with one other visitor, a very old lady. We are instructed how to pull a rope to toll a bell when we want to be let out. The old lady shows me how to look into a little mirror behind a tiny statue of Christ in a glass case. In the mirror you can see that his back is lacerated. There is a golden chalice with which Juan gave the nuns communion.  Many years later Pope John Paul II had come here and used it.  Most striking of all is a little picture Juan drew in pen and ink on a scrap of paper.  It represents a vision he had recently had.  It looks down from above and to one side onto Christ hanging dead on the cross.  The arms look almost dislocated. The torso arches away from the wood.  The knees are bent double.  The head hangs right down on to the breast.  The hands are torn by the nails.  Blood has dripped.  The whole sketch is set in an oval.  Less uncomfortable than this, and the thing I feel is closest to Juan, and close to me too, is the little chair Juan used to sit on with his ear to the grille, hearing confessions.  It has a worn leather seat.

Most of the museum is, of course, about Teresa,  And most of the town too.  The image of her that I hold in my head gradually seems to merge into and soften up the image I hold of Mrs Thatcher in my head.  Both forceful in reform, however hard for some the experience might turn out to be.

As I leave the enclosure I ask if I may visit Juan's little cottage by the wall.  No.  It has been dismantled, brought in and re-erected in rather better shape inside the enclosed garden, for the delight of the nuns.

It was to the cottage that a group of angry men came one early December night in 1577 to kidnap Juan.  Too long had the little reformed descalzo held the coveted post of confessor at the great unreformed convent of Encarnación, right under the noses of the unreformed friars in their monastery looking out over the city walls above.  Too long had his Christ-like example thrilled their nuns and provided such an obvious contrast with the conservative and political preoccupations of the more comfortable unreformed Carmelite establishment up on the hill.  The kidnappers were unreformed Carmelite fathers, lay Carmelite workers and armed mercenaries from the streets of Ávila.  They didn't knock but broke down the door.  The noise of it reached the nuns in the enclosure.

Juan held out his hands to be bound and was wrenched away into the darkness.  'Well and good', he said.  'Let us go'.  They scrambled and hauled him up the slope to the walls of the city.  Through the Puerta del Carmen and into the unreformed Carmelite monastery of the Observance.  Here waited the prior of the unreformed Carmelites of the rich, black-cobbled city of Toledo.  He was Padre Maldonado – evil-given.  He ordered that Juan should be whipped, in two separate short sessions, before being cast into a cell. And there he was to remain for two or three days.

During this time, he was allowed to attend mass in the monastery. At the end of one service he found himself carelessly left alone and he simply wandered off back down to Encarnación. He let himself into his cottage and began to tear up, and even eat, some letters and papers which he feared might be used to bring other descalzos, and perhaps Teresa, into as much trouble with the Carmelite Order as he found himself in. He was caught in the act and dragged back to his prison cell. A note in his hand-writing survived – 'el fin del alma es amar', the purpose of the soul is to love. It was time for Maldonado to remove him to the hard-hearted religious stronghold that was, and is, Toledo. They put him on a mule and led him off through snow and sleet.

I follow him, on foot without a mule and under a summer sky. I come into town from Encarnación, through the Puerta del Carmen. From this northern gate, I walk straight across town, some 500 yards to the southern gate which is now called Puerta de Santa Teresa, of course. Here a rather ugly little ecclesiastical complex stands on the site of the house in which she was born. Inside it is preserved one of her fingers. I see that it is still wearing a ring set with a large green stone. From here, I go steeply downhill and then, a kilometre out, I pass the bull-ring and head across the fertile plain towards the mountains.

As I walk southwards, the road, which I suppose to be the road to Toledo, becomes less and less frequented. At one point there is a queue of dilapidated cars and vans by the side of the road, waiting to enter a large wired off encampment enclosing a few large sheds. Some vehicles contain just a hefty tee-shirted driver. Some seem to contain whole families, There is a great deal of cigarette smoking but not much progress. Soon after leaving this enigma behind, the road starts to dwindle away. There is no traffic now. I realise that I am on the old winding road out of Ávila towards Toledo, a road without inns or people, the road Juan was probably taken on. I have covered about a league, about an hour in the right direction but on the wrong road for me. I need inns and people. I walk for an hour back into the city and ask a taxi-driver to take me my two wasted leagues south again for a fresh start on the new road. He drops me at mid-day, 4,500 feet up near the great pass of Puerto de la Paramera, the pass over the first range between Ávila and Toledo. It is cold and windy. The hills are magnificent, bare and rocky. A small hand-painted sign beside the road boasts that they breed toros bravos up here.

I have taken to the road again with a huge, chronic blister but I count my blessings. Paso a paso va lejos, step by step goes far. Juan's journey over these same hills was the mid-winter of his short life. He was exactly half the age I am now.

# 9  COMMENDED TO COLD OBLIVION

The afternoon sunshine blows coldly over me as I wind down the road from the steep pass of Paramera. The windy spaces all around, the wild slopes, the clear light of the hills in high summer, my steady pace downhill, this feels like freedom. My whereabouts are not known. 'In order to arrive at what you do not know, you must go by a way that you do not know,' as Juan said.

Juan rode through here on a mule in the half-light of a December day and the blind obscurity of a December night. Snow and sleet must have closed off any view of the hills and hidden the travellers from curious eyes. The cold must have bitten through his damp, threadbare cloak and habit. Hail must have lashed his bare feet and ankles. His wrists were bound. Padre Maldonado, prior of the calzos, the shod, the comfortably unreformed Carmelite priory of Toledo, rode in front. A mule driver urged the animals on. The single accompanying friar assisted progress by abusing and buffeting the prisoner. Nobody told Juan where he was or where he was going. This was extraordinary rendition.

Teresa did not know, and nor did any of the descalzo community scattered around Castile know, where the beloved confessor had disappeared to. He had simply been snatched out of their lives. Inside Spain and hid from sight.

For another page of Juan's own life was being turned. He was 35 years old, so this year was his third climacteric. At his first, at seven years old, the little boy had become 'viable', a survivor in his harsh, ill-furnished environment. At his second climacteric, at 21 he had become a man, man enough to make his own way in it. Now, at 35, he should have been entering his age of consolidation, settling himself and dependents around him. Indeed, the young friar, the confessor, would soon be exercising the paternal responsibilities of a prior. But first there was this painful rite of passage to endure.

Perhaps, paradoxically, Juan may have been actually experiencing his kidnapping as some sort of a release. Release from the pressures of his women, from the debilitation and the nightmares those pressures wrought in him. Release, also from the state of suspended animation he too often felt in himself, 'Then my life the same stand-by, of not dying I die'. Here now was a turn of events for him to make the most of. As Teresa had said, 'We are called to make a virtue of necessity'. Perhaps Juan actually felt that his seizure, his uprooting, provided a new opening for him, a new path, a new opportunity for love in the service of the eternal mystery that is God.

Five leagues out of Ávila, and over the pass, the road runs down as a long, straight street through the large village or small town of Barraco, big enough to have its own bullring. Here I stop, although Juan would almost certainly have been hurried on into the darkness.

A bar called 'El Chato' is run by a sharp but friendly young man, more townee than villager. He has a room he can let me have for the night in the building next door. He takes me to it up three flights of stone stairs, accompanied by a silent young woman whose role is not made clear. She leaves with him. The room is tiny, a closet. It is very cheap.

Chato can mean a small, stubby glass for wine. Its first meaning is snub as in snub-nosed in a face or small breasted in a woman. 'Chato', the muleteer would affectionately address his beast, rubbing its rounded snubby muzzle.

When I go into the bar to drink wine out of one of these miniscule, mule-muzzled, small breasted, snub-nosed glasses, the knowing proprietor hands me a small sheet of paper. It is covered in solid type, printed as if it were a political tract or a local appeal. It says: 'Esteemed colleagues, I am not guilty towards anyone for my death; I leave this life because if I lived two days more I would not know who I was in this sea of tears. Look Señor Judge: I had the disgrace of marrying a widow. Had I known it I would not have married, because she had a daughter, and my father who was a widower, as a major disgrace fell in love with the daughter of my wife: by manner of which my wife was mother-in-law of my father and, at the same time, he was my son-in-law. In a little while my new mother brought into the world a male, who was my brother but, at the same time was the grandson of my wife, by means of my being the grandfather of my brother. In the course of time my wife brought into the world a male and, as he was the brother of my mother, he was the brother-in-law of my father and the uncle of my father's son; my wife was mother-in-law of her

80

own son and I on the other hand, am father of my mother, my father and his wife are my children and, besides, I am my own grandfather. So look, Señor Judge: I despair of this world because I don't know who I am any more. (signed) The Dead Man'.

I spend the rest of the afternoon sitting on a stone step outside the church, translating this complaint and trying to disentangle the story of an unfortunate marriage.

A wedding party assembles in front of me and then enters the church. Guests, family, groom and bride. It all looks very old-fashioned, respectable and rather impoverished. Later they come out and hang around talking and taking photographs. When they notice me they are pleasant enough.

Two or three generations ago the priest in this church urged these catholic families to go out and kill Barraco's protestant community as 'sons of Satan' (Beevor. 'The Spanish Civil War').

In the morning I am on the road again with my blister now the size of a plover's egg and no breakfast from El Chato's proprietor, who perhaps stayed up late at the wedding feast.

I am still walking steadily down-hill into one of the rifts in the crumpled fault-line between Ávila and Toledo, the fault-line that separates the two great central Spanish plateaux. Old Castile to the north and New Castile to the south. This is a good road, a very open road. There are mountains to either side. The lower I go, the warmer the air. The sun breaks through.

Eventually the road runs beside a great stretch of water, man-made and modern. Juan's road must have run on down the valley floor, underwater now. At the end of this water I have to cross a high metal bridge over the outflow. Its walkway is narrow and the handrail is too low for comfort. Wearing my heavy backpack heightens my sense of vertigo.

Once across the water, I break out of mountain country and start to climb from the valley into hill country. I can see for miles. The tiny road twists and turns through grassy slopes scattered with occasional rocks and stunted oaks. Sometimes there are olive trees and sometimes little vineyards. Juan would have seen none of this in the darkness at the end of his first day on the road. I, on the other hand, find it delightful, and I struggle mentally with Juan's instruction to shut it all out and enter the dark night of the senses, to put nada in the place of nature.

After an easy half-day of not much more than four leagues up and down, I come into Cebreros, a small town on a Sunday afternoon. This is my second halt on the road from Ávila to Toledo. I think that Cebreros was probably Juan's first stopping place. In Cebreros, too, Isabel's cortege parked her coffin for the night on the long haul south towards Granada. For Juan and Isabel the winter storms were apocalyptic. My weather is benign. On my way into town I overtake an old man on a dirty white donkey, with saddlebags strung on each side and a bony hunting dog trotting along. The man's face is brown and leathery, impassive. This oldster is what they call a tostado here, a toasted one, straight out of Cervantes. Unlike Juan and Isabel, and me, the great Don never came this way.

Was it here, in Cebreros, that Juan was offered freedom and turned it down? By the end of the long day the young mule driver had developed a great sympathy for the much abused Juan. He was so worn down, frail and thin, so harshly treated and so patiently accepting of his treatment that one might fear for his survival. The mule driver urged the inn-keeper to observe the quiet virtue of the little man, the kindliness that his suffering could not extinguish. They asked him where his family lived and made a plan to spirit him away from his captors and lead him by secret paths over the mountains and all the way to Medina del Campo. Once Maldonado and his friar were asleep, the mule driver put the plan to Juan. He was grateful but refused. He must follow the path that God and the Carmelites seemed to be commending to him.

For me in Cebreros it is the Lord's day, Domingo. In Spain you simply can't get away from Sunday being The Lord's day. Every time you think of this day of the week, or mention it by name, there you have it, Domingo, Lord's day. All the families, all the generations, are hanging about in the pleasant square of Cebreros making a great chatter. All are in their Sunday best. There have been first communions made. Suddenly, in one corner of the square, there is a short burst of very loud firework explosions, and then rockets shoot up in a set, simultaneously, into the sky.

I find a hostal for the night. It is picturesque, with a pretty garden before the entrance. A film crew, or television, are recording something here. A beautiful young model is waiting to walk up to the hostal door as I lurch sweatily past, pack on back staff in hand. The innkeeper installs me in a ground floor room with shutters and takes my money. He explains that I am his only customer tonight and that when the film crew has gone he is going to lock up the hostal from the outside, with me inside. In the morning, 'James', for he likes saying my name and attaches it to every phrase he utters, in the morning all I have to do is to open my shutters, 'James,' and jump out, 'James,' into the flowerbed. Which I do.

So another start without benefit of breakfast. And because it is early it is, of course, cold up here in these lovely hills. My first unexpected encounter is with a small dead scorpion lying in the dust beside the road. It seems like a warning not to wander off the strait and narrow.

I am winding downhill between woods but I am not convinced that the road I am on is the one I had in mind for today. A short conversation with a helpful old boy, another tostado like me, trying to start his van, reassures me that this is the only road, so I carry on into the brightening morning.

After a few hours, a few wooded leagues, I come down into a lowland stretch through green pastures with stone walls and shady trees, not typically Castilian in style, more Irish, very pretty.

The best moment of the day comes in early afternoon when I come to the four prehistoric stone bulls, the toros de Guisando, standing untended beside the quiet road like four fat torpedos. Here in 1468 the king, Henry IV of Castile y Leon, acknowledged his 17-year-old sister Isabel as his heir. She would go on to create, for the first time, a unified Spain, the country that survives to this day. And here in 1577 Juan was led past, hands bound, on a mule. I wonder if he noticed the bulls. He would pass this way as a free man several times over the coming years, happily. To leave the road and pat the bulls I have to pass through no gate, have to present myself at no ticket kiosk, have to buy coffee in no cafeteria, have to browse through no souvenir shop. No cars even pass while I am here. 'Y los toros de Guisando, casi muerte y casi piedra, and the bulls of Guisando, all but death and all but stone,' as Lorca put it.

Along the road towards me comes my mirror image, backpack, staff, shorts, sandals, red face, grey crop. He is a German and he is walking on a pilgrimage to Santiago de Compostela from Alicante. This is his fifth time to the tomb of Spain's national saint, Santiago, St James the Greater, Christ's disciple. He is an obsessive who would like to cover it off from every point of the compass. Now is the turn of the south-east. We exchange notes. I too am a pilgrim. I walked to Compostela, once, not from Alicante but from Paris.

Soon after this I pass a man ploughing behind his mule between his vines. Man, mule and plough look well worn but effective. Like me, and like the German pilgrim, he is walking all day  Although he just walks back and forth over the same ground he is getting somewhere. He stops to talk. Both he and his mule seem to be positive and sociable characters.

From start to finish, this day's road passes not one village, not one café, not one bar.

Finally I come to a very steep climb, zigzagging with hairpin bends. On the ridge at the top is the small town of Cadalso de los Vidrios. Cadalso means a high place and Vidrios means glass, crystal or window panes. When Juan came through, this place was famous for its glass making. Now its industry is granite and gravel and it is not famous any more.

Clearly ancient, obviously picturesque, Cadalso de los Vidrios feels grim. It is sombre although the sol shines. There is no plaza for humanity to flower in. The streets seem to lead asymmetrically nowhere. It is a place of indoor people.  The innkeeper where I stay is an impatient fellow, impatient with my uncertainty but impatient for what?

I am happy to be afoot again, unbreakfasted, early the next morning. The wind is blowing hard into my back from the north. Cadalso, on its ridge, is so exposed to north and south that in midwinter here Juan must have had to call on all  his powers of negation of the senses.
Downhill and through woods again I come into the region of La Mancha, named from the Arabic word for a dry plateau. And with the most famous character in Spanish literature named for the region. Man of La Mancha. Unlike most of Quixote's wandering days, my first day in La Mancha is quite uneventful.

After nearly three hours, three leagues, 15 kilometres, I walk through my first village. Its name is Almorox, as if it were a brand of stock cube or an air-freshener.

The road at last comes out of the hills into a plain or, rather, a high plateau again, burnt brown and yellow and, this far south, already harvested. Two men digging a ditch take my unusual appearance as a good excuse to stop work for a few minutes and have a nice chat with me about what I am doing walking down the road past their ditch. They are much interested in me and Juan.

The creature of the day is the snake. I give myself a great fright by almost stepping on one that is writhing about, badly damaged, in my path. Later there is another one, quite dead.

Finally, in early afternoon, I come through fertile looking country into Escalona. The name has some connotation of terracing. The town sits on a small table of higher ground. It was once walled but it has sloughed this skin off now. I am surprised to find in the centre a great wreck of a castle, square, massive and shattered. Apparently the court of the Duke of Escalona here was once one of the most magnificent in Spain. Now the town feels run down. Several small business premises are empty and for sale.

If you wanted to remove yourself as far as possible, all at the same time, from the fine restaurants of San Sebastian and Santander, from the aesthetics of Barcelona, from the teeming beaches and fashions of the Costas from the romance of Andalusia, from the ocean gateways of Cadiz and Corunna, and even from the bones of Spain's patron saint in Compostela, then Escalona would be the place for you. At least 100 leagues, 100 hours walking, to get to any of the busy commercial fringes of Spain from this out of commission Castilian dead centre.

Juan probably stopped here during his second night of bondage and bitter cold on the road into the dark.

I sit over a drink in the old-fashioned, small town square and make notes. The barman asks me if I am writing 'en inglés o en castellano'. No mention of 'español'.

Later I find a bar with rooms. The suspicious proprietor shows me to a room with four single, metal-frame beds in it. I am to use the bar-room clientele's washroom. He shows me how I am to let myself out, unbreakfasted, through his own front door in the morning while he sleeps on.

This extraordinary modern fashion, or mannerism, among the Spanish of rising late – every rural village street is deserted until nearly ten in the morning – lunching at half-past-two and dining an hour before midnight, arose only in the twentieth century. It is an infernal nuisance to wayfarers.

I rise early the next morning and quietly find my way to mine host's front door. The key is in the lock, the hall is bare except for one small table. The only thing on the table is a large pistol, looking clean, oiled and well-maintained. I resist the temptation to pick it up. I set off down the street with both feet burning in my sandals.

It is only five leagues of road, fairly flat, fairly straight, fairly well-used, fairly dull, from Escalona to Torrijos. For me this is a nada stretch. I use it to think about Juan's nada of the spirit. Perhaps he too was thinking about it when he was coming along here.

Juan wrote that achieving nada of the spirit was even more difficult than achieving nada of the senses. Switching off all one's senses and entering into a dark nothingness of the senses, detached from any feeling of living in oneself or in one's physical surroundings, can be a beneficial accomplishment – particularly so when in painful circumstances. Through mental will-power one's senses can be quenched. But how to put one's spirit totally to rest, how to switch off the spirit, how to turn that light out?

It is difficult, but it is worth doing, said Juan. Only thus will one's soul get anywhere. 'The soul journeys, so to speak, by night, in darkness'. The love of God cannot enter into a soul that is busy with spiritual fancies. The more the spirit withdraws itself completely from all figures of the imagination about God, the closer to God it will be. One has to try, and it is difficult, to stop one's spirit from being in any way active or in any way desirous of any kind of spiritual understanding. We must learn to be still and spiritually empty even though we think we are doing nothing, nada. As for our will, all we should do is ground it in humble love. Virtue does not consist in perceptions and feelings about God, it consists in a deeply rooted state of humility and spiritual poverty, said Juan. This message of Juan's about spiritual poverty suddenly makes sense for me of the words of a beatitude that I had always previously found puzzling: 'Blessed are the poor in spirit; for theirs is the kingdom of heaven'.

Only from the darkness at the bottom of a deep well can a man look up and see the stars of heaven shine in their full glory.

Anyway, with my blisters and my anxious questing, my own restlessness is a very long way from the stillness of Juan's dark night of the senses and his dark night of the spirit, let alone from the kingdom of heaven.

I come through vast olive groves into Torrijos and find it a bustling and modernising sort of a town. I walk round in circles in the centre, looking for somewhere to stay, and I get lost, eventually fetching up against a magnificently ornate church portico.

This turns out to be the very same great collegiate church that Juan's mother carried him to, all the way from Fontiveros, down the road I have been walking, when he was two years old. These are the very same church steps from which the rich uncle, the archdeacon, turned the destitute young mother and child away. That was a horrid moment. But now, on this occasion, today, the opposite happens. A young woman with a small child sees that I am lost, and at a loss, and they take me in hand and they lead me several hundred yards through the streets to a hotel – rather better than I am used to. So, just where an impoverished young mother and child in great need were turned away to misery, another young mother and child have led a rich man in no great need to comfort and shelter. It would be nice to think that she gets commission for this helpful service.

I like Torrijos. It is the same kind of re-built town as Medina del Campo, with the same kind of friendly people ready to humour the only potty old traveller in town. In the tourist office, it says of itself that it has cold winters and short, dry, very hot summers. Welcome to Castile. Vegetation is profuse in aromatic plants – thyme, fennel, rosemary, etc. Fauna is 'poco relevante' (a little notable), with an abundance of hares, rabbits and partridges which have great cinegético (hunting) value.

This same tourist office does not know that Juan was ever in Torrijos, and doesn't know much about him at all. Nor does anyone else I talk to here.

I wonder if Juan knew where he was when he was led through here a prisoner, probably in the dark, and whether he thought of his previous unhappy visit, as an infant. He would surely not be able to remember an experience he had had at the age of only two.

I follow a knife sharpener along the street. He is pushing his bicycle tool of the trade. He has a sort of wooden pan-pipe on which he plays a short, piercing tune outside each house. Presumably it is his signature tune or advertising jingle. But nobody comes out.

At eight o'clock in the evening I go to mass in the great church. As the service progresses, the number of old ladies present steadily increases to about 40. the number of old men remains stuck at three of us. In the great cage of choir stalls behind me there are the splendid marble effigies of a nobleman and his wife. Not the sort of images I suppose that Juan would have found to be 'of great benefit for remembering God'. More like vanity. Perhaps they were distant relations of the cruel archdeacon.

And so to bed, for tomorrow is Toledo. There is a small, dead, black bat on my windowsill.

In the morning I am on the move well breakfasted, for a change.

The road towards Toledo starts off very straight. To either side are stretches of yellow and brown. There is already a heat haze in the air, although the sun has been up little more than an hour. After a while, the plain begins to heave like a great ocean swell.

Juan was heading, through bitter cold and darkness, towards a city that accommodated 1,400 men and women in religious orders. It was the head-quarters of The Spanish Inquisition. The spider's web was spun out from here to every furthest hamlet of the great kingdom. Teresa now had an inkling of Juan's fate. 'I would rather see him with the Moors', she said.

The Inquisition was the most powerful organ in Spain. The Inquisitor General was so powerful that he had even arrested the archbishop of Toledo himself, the highest cleric in the land. This poor man had died the year before Juan was seized, after seventeen years of incarceration for suggested heresy (Green). And, soon after, the Inquisitor General himself became also Archbishop of Toledo, Primate of Spain and a Cardinal (Lynch). His income was second only to the king's. the two powers, spiritual and temporal, went hand in hand. The Spanish Inquisition was a closer partner to the Spanish Crown than it was to the Church of Rome (Baigent, 'The Inquisition'). Their chief joint objective was wealth. The property of persons convicted of heresy was confiscated and paid into the Crown, who returned part of it to the church (Brenan, 'The Face of Spain').

But the addiction of the Inquisition itself, its intoxication, its particular poison, was its compulsion for control. In 1578, the year Juan would spend in a cell in Toledo, an Inquisitor wrote, 'We must remember that the main purpose of the trial and execution is not to save the soul of the accused but to achieve the public good and put fear into others'. The story is told of the Grand Inquisitor who said, 'The most tormenting secrets of their conscience – everything, everything they will bring to us, and we shall give them our decision for it all, and they will be glad to believe in our decision, because it will relieve them of their great anxiety, and of their present terrible torments of coming to a free decision themselves. And they will all be happy.' (Dostoevsky, 'The Brothers Karamazov').

Mystics were seen to be people out of control, so Juan's case was already being examined by the intelligence bureaux of the Inquisition in Valladolid and Toledo itself before ever he reached that city. Throughout his life, examinations by the Inquisition of his writings, his reported sayings and his reported behaviour would continue at regular intervals.

What made the Inquisition's grip on the Spanish people so inexorable was its intelligence network and its bureaucratic system. Every case file was up-to-date and in good order, and fresh information was constantly being added to it.

Some 20,000 'familiars' of the Inquisition were scattered throughout Spain to listen for, and to inform on, unorthodoxy. There might be 50 in a town, two in a small village. There was a climate of fear and suspicion. Four years before Juan's arrest the Venetian Ambassador had reported, 'Such is the fear that everyone has of this tribunal that no-one talks about or enquires into its proceedings very much for fear of becoming himself in any way an object of suspicion.' (Casey).

The countless unpaid familiars could find their reward in immunity to ordinary civil jurisdiction and in freedom to commit crimes beyond reach of the law (Hume).

Anyone could denounce anyone else and the burden of vindication would lie with the accused.  People increasingly began to fear their neighbours, their professional associates, their competitors, and indeed anyone who might be bearing a grudge, anyone whom they might have antagonised (Baigent).

Those arrested were not told what evidence there was against them nor who had accused them.  In this nightmare of ignorance, fear and overwhelming power, sexual submission might be blackmailed out of women vainly hoping to get their husbands or lovers out of the torturers' hands (Green).

For torture was the dynamic that animated the interrogation process. Once the suspect was safely in chains, in solitary confinement in prison within one of the Inquisition's 21 provincial palaces, the process was simply to extract the required confession.  And more important than confessing his own transgressions was confessing evidence to incriminate others.

The Inquisition's men in holy orders would not, themselves, lay a finger on the accused.  Instead, the local public executioner would be called in and paid half an ounce of gold for each session.  The windowless interrogation cell would be lit by lanterns.  The  Inquisitors would sit on chairs to ask their questions. The torturer would be masked, only his eyes showing. The prisoner would be naked.  Every detail, every word, every action would be noted and recorded for the file.

First the prisoner would be told that if he should be injured, mutilated, or even die, this would be his own responsibility, for not telling the required truth.  And the Inquisition recognised that a confession extracted during torture was not in itself valid.  It would become valid only when the victim confirmed and ratified it the next day.

The Inquisition's own rules allowed the suspect to be tortured only once, so the end of each session was declared to be not the end but the 'suspension'.

The techniques used seemed, in theory, to be designed to keep actual bloodshed to a minimum. They were the rack (potro), thumbscrew (empulgueras), pulley (garrucha) and water torture (toca).

Once the required confession had been extracted, the victim could languish unmolested in solitary confinement until the day of his punishment in a great, colourful celebration called an act of faith, an auto de fe. In Juan's day the great majority of guilty victims were not executed but simply reduced to public humiliation and penury (their home and all possessions having been visited, listed and valued on the day of their arrest, in preparation for appropriation on the day of their act of faith). Those who were executed, mainly unrepentant heretics, lapsed conversos and practising Jews, were burned alive, although those who recanted of their heresy might first be mercifully strangled at the stake, and those who had already died might be dug up to be burned, or might be burned in effigy.

Once again bloodshed was avoided, this time through the use of fire as the supreme instrument. The Inquisitor of Seville said that he saw it as his mission, 'to burn and embrace people'.

The autos de fe functioned as mass theatres of power. Above them stood the Inquisition's symbol, a green cross decorated with green foliage, living faith as opposed to the dead wood which would be burnt. The guilty were clad in yellow sackcloth decorated with demonic images. This sinister garment with pointed hood was called a sanbenito, a St Benedict. They would be led into the town's great square, which would often be furnished with temporary grandstands. At their head was a monk carrying a crucifix veiled in black crepe. The victims came in a long column, two by two, barefoot, each carrying an extinct candle. Following them came a long file of monks singing psalms. There would be a mass, with a sermon. Then the civil authorities carried out the burnings. The Inquisitors, the religious, must not be sullied (Erlanger 'Isabelle la Catholique'). All this was done in front of a great crowd.

Juan de la Cruz was, of course, not being carried off to Toledo by the Inquisition. But his Carmelite captors were legitimised by being able to share the culture of the Inquisition, the culture of intolerance, secrecy, brutality, power and control, whose heart-beat of darkness reverberated so loudly in their city.

As I follow the road south and east, the tawny swell of the land begins to break up into earthworks of deep, blood red. There are bushy ravines. From more than a league away I can already see the great, squared-off Alcázar, the fortress, rising above the city. It is an impressive sight and forbidding. But the outskirts are long and drearisome.

Juan came into the old city through the Puerta de Bisagra, the great gate of the hinge. There is enough room between its inner and outer walls to put two companies of soldiers on parade. After three December days and nights of biting cold, Juan was led through here on his mule, bound and blindfolded, and in darkness. He was so much in the dark. He was about to disappear into a black hole. Toledo. But he was always at home in the dark night.

I follow Juan through the Bisagra gate, deeply prejudiced. This city makes my heart sink.

# 10 IN THE TOILS OF TOLEDO

The Toledo that Juan was dragged into was the richest and most priest-ridden city in Spain. It represented the very spirit of Spanish Catholicism, its great stone towers erected on the ashes of its defeated Muslim rivals (Crastre, 'Toledo'). Yet all over town, beneath the palaces and churches, beside the streets and squares, impoverished families scraped out their household pittances in cellars and caves. One in nine of Toledo's 50,000 population lived in holes below the surface level of Toledo's great civilisation (Christian).

By the rules of geography Toledo belonged to Castile. Never mind. Toledo would be different. It has always been an island in the old map of Spain (Barea, 'The Clash').

The unreformed Carmelite priory that Juan was brought to was the Order's grandest establishment in Spain. Eighty friars lived there under the leadership of prior Maldonado, who must have been delighted to return to his home comforts after three bitter days and nights on the road with Juan. And it would soon be Christmas.

The façade looked towards Toledo's busy main square, Plaza Zocodover, Zoco from the Arabic word souk, meaning market. To one side was the great Alcázar, the fortress that dominated the city and still does. At the back, the priory was protected by the fast flowing Tagus, the Rio Tajo. Juan was to be stuck here, within the stone walls of this conservative Carmelite monastery, for eight months. Nine months could well have killed him.

He was immediately stripped of his humble descalzo habit and forced into an ample habit of the fine cloth of the calzos. It was probably too big for his tiny frame, which must have been even more wasted and shrunken than usual by the terrible journey following immediately on from his rough treatment and two whippings in Ávila. He must have looked a little pathetic, even absurd, in his new outfit. He was to be tried now by a tribunal led by the city prior, Maldonado, and a national Carmelite heavyweight, Tostado.

The evil given and the toasted one sound like characters from a grim fairy story. But first he had to stand in front of all the assembled friars of the monastery as an exhibit of wrongdoing, a curiosity to be mocked and insulted. How was he feeling? Well, he seemed, for once, not to be seeking refuge in nada, nothing, the night of the senses and the night of the spirit, for his arguments in self-defence were bright, focussed and firm.

The toasted one had brought a document that claimed the authority of the pope to remove from office and punish all those reformed descalzos who had set themselves up in monasteries, or taken up other official positions, without the permission of the calzos, the unreformed, ruling Carmelite Order. This document was read out, probably to much nodding of heads from the assembled friars.

Juan pointed out that these sanctions did not apply to him. He had been given his appointment as confessor to the women in Encarnación through all the proper Carmelite channels. There were some labyrinthine bureaucratic and hierarchic constructs and clauses to be argued through. Juan argued them. He was also able to make a telling reference to the support of the Royal Council, which Teresa had obtained. Tostado was uncomfortably aware that the letters concerning his own authority under the pope, letters which he had himself presented to the king of Spain had been rejected as invalid by the Royal Council just six weeks earlier.

To Tostado, Juan was a rebel. In the words of Tostado's document, Juan was one of those 'disobedient, rebellious and contumacious' descalzo friars who must repent of their 'fallacies, cavilling and misrepresentations' and simply accept the calzo Carmelite authority (Casey).

Tostado, not having been able to win the argument about how his papal document applied to Juan, resorted to physical threats. Juan replied that he would not yield one inch on this matter, even though it should cost him his life. So the toasted one tried the opposite tack. Juan would be made a prior somewhere nice, with a good library. No. A cross of precious metal. No. Tostado even tried a bribe of pieces of gold. The little descalzo responded, 'A man who is seeking Christ in absolute poverty has no need of golden trinkets'.

The tribunal decided that it had tried hard enough. It declared Juan was a rebel and contumacious, contemptuous of Carmelite authority. Tostado sentenced him to imprisonment without setting a time limit on it.

For two months Juan disappeared into the priory's general purpose prison cell. But this was obviously not secure enough for such a high-risk offender.

On a freezing February day, Juan was thrown into his own, special, customised lock-up. It was so uncomfortable that it was a full-time punishment, in itself, just to be there. It was a closet, a large recess in the stone walls of the monastery. In a Kafka-esque way, it opened off the monastery's guest bedroom for visiting friars. Had it been used as their clothes cupboard? Travelling monks don't have much in the way of clothes in their luggage. More likely it had been their lavatory. It was certainly foul enough.

Juan found it to be about six feet wide by ten feet long, with no window but a small opening, three fingers wide, high up in the end wall. On the floor were some boards and two old blankets. Also a bucket for hygienic purposes. It was dark and smelly in there and it would get smellier. After two months already in prison, Juan's habit was worn and dirty. Lice bred in it. His skin bled. The terrible cold up here in the wall of the monastery soon had his toes peeling with frostbite. With all the muck came dysentery.

Juan was not entirely devoid of human company. Every day the friar appointed as his gaoler put food and drink on the floor for him. Four days a week Juan had bread, water and a sardine, or sometimes half a sardine. Three days a week he fasted on bread and water. Every now and again the gaoler took his bucket away to empty it. He never spoke to Juan.

On Mondays, Wednesdays and Fridays, Juan actually joined Maldonado and the assembled friars down in their refectory. While they sat to eat at table, Juan knelt to eat his bread and water from the stone floor. When supper was finished, Maldonado would stand over him to upbraid him harshly. He was a hypocrite. He had become descalzo only in order to be thought a saint. This pride of his had thrown the whole Order into confusion. 'And who is he? A wretched little friar like him to cause us all this disturbance!' Once a week this was followed by what was called the circular discipline. Juan had to pull his habit down from his shoulders and his back and then walk round the table. Each friar, as he passed, struck him with a cane. Did each bring his own cane or was there one cane passed from hand to hand?  Anyway, each blow drew blood, and the previous week's wounds were soon open again.  It was no wonder his habit became so foul.  During the circular discipline, the friars sang the fifty-first psalm: 'Have mercy upon me, O God, according to thy loving kindness:  according unto the multitude of thy tender mercies.'  Juan probably sang it with them.  Other than that, he said nothing.

On days when they didn't have the pleasure of Juan's company at their supper, some of the friars would gather outside Juan's cell and talk at him through the locked door.  The descalzos were being suppressed, they said.  Reform was over and done with.  Perhaps they should dispose of Juan down a well.  No-one would know.

Left alone in his cell he worried about Teresa and the descalzos.  He worried that they might think he had given up, walked out on them.  Perhaps he really should give up.  Was he descalzo for the wrong reasons?  Were the calzo fathers right?  In his dark night of the senses and his dark night of the spirit, the state of nada, nothing, that he achieved was, it seems, not much visited by consolations from God.  That would have been a rare thing, he said later.  And that to have received a single grace from God would have compensated for years in prison (Sesé).

In thinking about himself and his situation, there was a thought that he might be being punished for having previously imposed unnecessary privations on himself, one of God's creatures after all – punished by Toledo imposing even more severe privations to teach him a lesson (Stinissen. 'Découvre-moi Ta présence').  Certainly, once free and a prior with authority over others, his first concern, wherever he went, would be to cut down on penitential exercises and to relieve burdens and trials.  He would give more time for recreation and introduce more tender, loving care.  He would focus himself 'on one thing only, which is to love.'

Neither in prison or out did Juan ever find it within himself to resent his treatment or to blame Maldonado and his men.  If, later, people became indignant about what had been done to him, the most he would allow to be said about the matter was that 'they did it because they did not understand'.  Juan's job was to teach Christians how to be Christian.  Even in the monastery in Toledo he was doing this.  Some of the uncorrupted young friars, novices and students were deeply moved by the gentle humility with which Juan bore the insults and blows of the elders. Some were moved to tears, saying, 'This man is a saint, they can say what they like'.

One consolation that did come to Juan in the darkness of his cell was poetry; beauty and order where all else was ugliness and disorder. Not anymore the wordily contrived negativism of 'I live not in me...Of not dying I die', but now a positive, lyrical mysticism. He was finding his voice.

Day and night the sound of running water came to Juan from the rocky bed of the Tagus below the priory. It became his muse. One of the first poems that he sang in his head gave meaning to the stream, his constant companion. He called it 'Song of the soul that rests itself in knowing God through faith'.

> The stream, I know well, courses past,
> Although it is night.
>
> This river, hid from sight,
> I know to run deep and fast,
> Although it is night.
>
> Its origin no-one knows,
> From the source of all things it flows,
> Although it is night.
>
> Nothing can be so fair,
> And skies and earth drink there,
> Although it is night.
>
> No finding there of ground,
> No crossing ever found,
> Although it is night.
>
> Its brightness never emptied away,
> From it comes all the light of day,
> Although it is night.

I know its current so bountiful,
Waters heaven and hell and us people,
Although it is night.

The current that is born from that spring,
I know so well can do everything,
Although it is night.

Fount and issue, the two proceed
As one flood nothing can precede,
Although it is night.

In that eternal font, so concealed,
Bread to give life is revealed,
Although it is night.

Here is that calling out to all creatures,
To fill themselves to the last drop from these waters,
Because it is night.

The living source that I yearn,
In bread of life I discern,
Although it is night.

With the end of the Castilian freezing invierno and the arrival of the Castilian stifling inferno, small acts of kindness began to come to Juan. His taciturn warder was replaced by a young Carmelite father, fresh in Toledo. This man sometimes omitted, as if forgetfully, to take Juan down to the refectory for his beating. His prisoner teased him gently: 'Father, why have they deprived me of what I merit?' A quiet and careful relationship developed. The young warder brought a clean tunic and took away Juan's foul rags. Juan asked him for paper, pen and ink. For an hour or so in the middle of the day enough light came in through the little opening high up in the wall for Juan to note down thoughts, meditational sayings, fragments of verse.

Juan's next poem was about himself in exile, above the running river again, a simple ballad paraphrasing Psalm 137 about the Jews in exile by the waters of Babylon. In translation I have matched his number of stresses per line, in this case three, and his rhyme scheme. I have refused to allow myself to shift any word or thought out of the line Juan put it in, even to make composition easier for myself. I want the translation to follow the order of his thought process, line by line. I have not, of course, been able to match the beauty of his phrases in sixteenth century Castilian.

Above the running rivers
That in Babylon I found,
I sat me down to weeping,
Watering the ground.

Bringing you to mind,
Oh Sion I loved so well
Sweet was your memory,
And with it more tears fell.

I put off festal clothes,
Workday ones I wore,
And I hung up on green willow
The harp that there I bore.

Placing it in hope
Of what in you I expected;
There love gave me a wound,
And there my heart extracted.

I asked him to kill me,
So sore was my due:
I put me in his fire,
To burn up I knew.

Absolving the young fledgling
That died by fire too;
In my state of dying,
I breathed in only you.

For you I was dying,
And for you I was reviving,
In that your memory
Was life giving as well as depriving.

Happy were the strangers
Whom I sat among.
They asked me to sing
What in Sion I had sung;
'Sing us a hymn of Sion,
Let us hear the song'.

I said: 'How in exile,
Where for Sion I am sad,
Shall I sing the joy
That in my Sion bade?
I would cast it to oblivion
If in exile I were glad'.

And may my palate stick
To the tongue with which I tell,
If I forget about you,
In the land where I now dwell.

Sion, by green branches
In Babylon my due,
May my right hand forget me,
Foremost in love of you,

If I do not remember,
What I most appreciated,
And if I were to be festive,
And without you celebrated.

Oh you daughter of Babylon,
In misery bereaved,
Fortunate was he
In whom I believed,
Who must return the punishment
I from your hand received.

And he shall gather his children,
With me, as in you I cried,
To the rock that is Christ
For whom I put you aside.

There is a touch of vengeance in the penultimate verse but, to be fair to Juan, it is there in the penultimate verse of the original psalm. And the last verse Juan has converted from Old Testament strife to New Testament salvation. The original says, 'Happy shall he be that taketh and dasheth thy little ones against the stones.'

With things looking up for Juan, I go in search of his place of detention. I find I can walk right through it. It is thin air, which I breathe in. Where the priory stood is an open space. Four roads meet here. Heading towards the river I find a plaque set high up in a stone wall, perhaps the remains of the old city wall. The plaque says that it is Toledo's 1968 tribute to San Juan de la Cruz, first Carmelite descalzo. It also carries five lines of his poetry, composed somewhere behind the wall which carries the plaque.

> On a dark night,
> I am burning with longings to love,
> Chance of delight!
> Unseen, on the move,
> With my house all quiet above.

It was time for Juan to be unseen, on the move, with his house all quiet above.

It was August. His closet was an oven. He was ill and he was on a starvation diet. Unless he used the last of his failing strength to escape he would die here. He must go out and continue God's work. He was already drawing up the first three of nine simple educational poems to set out the story of the coming of Christ, from 'In the beginning was the Word' to 'The Birth', 'Romances', as he called them.

He didn't just need to escape to survive. He was now driven to it by strong interior impulses for flight. It seemed that the motive was 'Thy will be done'. He made a plan.

First he must locate his cell in relation to the rest of the monastery and the outside world. He had only ever left it after dark to go down to be beaten in the refectory. In order to be able to make a recce, he offered to take his own stinking bucket to the latrines himself. His new gaoler agreed to this, unlocking his door when all the friars were safely asleep after lunch.

He left his closet and went out through the guest bedroom into a corridor. This was like a high, elevated cloister with great open arches looking towards the river, and with monastery yards below. There was a wooden beam along its parapet.

Next he obtained scissors, needle and thread from his kind warden. He put together a very long thread and tied a stone to the end. Out with his bucket to empty again, he let the thread down from the corridor to measure the drop. Back in his cell he tore his two thin blankets into strips and attached them end to end. Fortunately he was so frail that they would support him – down to a level about twice his height from the ground.

Over the days, while his door was unlocked for bucket duty, he was able to weaken the fittings for the padlock, working at two large screws until they became loose enough to push out from inside.

On the 14th August Juan was kneeling in his cell, forehead to the floor, rump to the door, when Maldonado suddenly came in and applied his boot. The prior wanted to know what his mind was on, face down like that. Juan replied that he had been thinking about the next day's mass for the Assumption to Heaven of the Blessed Virgin Mary, and of how much he would love to attend. 'Not while I'm here', said Maldonado. The escape was on.

It was a hot night and there was a setback in the shape of the arrival of two considerable Carmelite visitors to spend the night in the guest bedroom. They pushed their beds over to the open door giving onto the corridor to afford them some air. At two in the morning they were snoring steadily enough for Juan to make his move. He pushed out the screws of the lock on his door. They fell with a small clatter. 'Deo gratis, who is it?' called out one of the fathers. Did they know they had a saint lurking in their closet? When the snoring resumed, Juan crept out holding his blanket strips and an iron lamp-hook that he had been able to put by.

Out in the corridor, the high open cloister, Juan snagged the lamp-hook under the wooden parapet and tied his makeshift rope to it. He took off his habit and threw it over. Then he made the sign of the cross and down he went. He reached the end and let go. He fell onto a heap of stones, work in progress on repairing the city walls above the river. He put his habit back on, turned left, north, in the dark, along the city wall until he could drop down into a small yard. There was only one door in the walls of this yard, straight ahead of him. To his anguish, he realised that the yard was part of the convent of the nuns of the Concepción, neighbours of his Carmelite captors. What a sinful scandal to be found in this enclosure. With his last feeble reserves of energy he somehow managed to climb out and drop into an alleyway. Uphill away from the river he went, and came to the market square known as Zocodover.

Four hundred and thirty years later I find the convent of the Concepción without any difficulty. Of course I cannot go in but I can admire its stone walls, its fine brick tower and its old tiled roofs. Unlike most Carmelite, and particularly descalzo, establishments, it has not been bulldozed away.

I follow Juan up to the Zocodover. It has a McDonalds. Groups of tourists are being led around and parties of school children, with cardboard buckets of Coca Cola. Their coaches are parked up a side street leading to the grim Alcázar. This is the least attractive square I have yet walked through in Spain. As Brenan said in 'The Face of Spain', 'And so soon we got tired of looking at this dull little square'.

Poor Juan, so bruised and exhausted that he could barely walk, blundered into the Zocodover at some time before three in the morning of what would be a market day. There was a tavern still open. Late revellers called to him to join them. Market women dozing under their stalls noticed the tiny, barefoot, half-dressed friar and amused themselves by calling out to him with lewd suggestions until he was lost from sight. What he was looking for was the convent of the descalzas, Teresa's reformed Carmelite nuns. It was not far away but he had only ever been on the streets of Toledo blindfolded. If anybody directed him, he must have left the Zocodover to walk along a narrow street called Sillería, the chairmaker. When I follow Juan along the Sillería there are no chairmakers but fine buildings, restaurants, antiques and souvenirs. Eventually Juan found the door of a nobleman's house open, caballero and servant watching him from the porch. He asked if he might lie down on the stone bench there. They let him in and locked up.

In the morning Juan suffered the usual problem of the wayfarer in Spain – nobody up yet, no breakfast, door resolutely locked. There was no window for him to climb out of. He was trapped. The Carmelite hue and

103

cry would be on his tracks. He must find sanctuary with the nuns, the descalzas. He hammered on the hall door of the porch until a sleepy servant came and opened up to let him out. He asked the way from the first people he met and within minutes he was knocking at the door of the convent.

I follow him again down the Sillería and turn right as he must have done down a street now called Nuñez de Arce. The convent of San José was in a small square somewhere down here. But I don't find it. The bulldozers have hidden it.

For Juan, the only safe refuge from his pursuers would be inside the enclosure with the women, entry forbidden to men. The prioress decided that since a sick nun had asked for a priest to hear her confession it was not just permissible but urgent and essential that Juan should come in. Three keys were produced, each the responsibility of a different nun, the triple lock was opened and Juan was inside.

Within minutes the calzos were at the door asking after Juan. 'It would be a miracle if you were to see any friar here', they were told in truth. Patrols were sent out, eventually as far as Ávila and Medina del Campo. His young gaoler was reduced to the lowest rank of the Carmelite Order and condemned to silence in Chapter. But he must have inwardly rejoiced.

Throughout the morning the nuns fussed over Juan to the best of their ability. They were shocked at the state of him. They brought him pears cooked in cinnamon. They cleaned and tidied his habit. They wrapped him in an old black coat that had belonged to their chaplain. In the afternoon they locked the street door of their church and Juan sat there in the half darkness, leaning against an iron grill and dictating his verses to nuns on the other side. They said that 'to hear him was heavenly joy.'

Juan would not be able to stay the night in the convent. The prioress sent a message to a friend who was a canon of the cathedral and was also the administrator of the Hospital Santa Cruz, in which he had his own accommodation. His name was Mendoza and it was his family, three generations back, that had funded the building and equipping of the hospital. Now it was a general hospital for non-contagious ailments and for foundling children. It stood as a close neighbour to the Carmelite monastery in which Juan had been incarcerated for the last eight months.

Mendoza came round in a closed carriage and smuggled Juan away in it, still wrapped up in the chaplain's old black coat. Within minutes they were in the hospital. It seems that the angry, unreformed Carmelites never thought to look for Juan in the hospital, for he stayed there building his strength up, right under their noses for nearly two months.

Unlike the monastery, the hospital still stands. It is now a museum. I buy a ticket and go in. The central courtyard, arcaded all the way round on two stories, is one of the most beautiful spaces I have ever found myself in. Slender white pillars hold up broad, rounded arches. The first floor balustrade is of white stone pierced by hundreds of cruciform openings each in its own stone frame. In the courtyard stands a well, a small olive tree and some ornamental shrubs. Stone pathways intersect triangles and squares of grass.

The museum rooms that open off the courtyard mostly contain paintings. There are quite a few by el Greco. The artist was born a year before Juan and arrived in Toledo two years before him. The city treated the two men very differently. On arrival, el Greco was immediately commissioned to produce paintings for the cathedral. A long succession of orders would follow. He never needed to leave (Barrès. 'Greco ou le Secret de Tolede').

Having looked around and found no mention of Juan having ever been here, I provocatively ask the two ladies who seem to be managing the place who they think the hospital's most eminent patient has been. They know nada. When I name Juan they still look blank. A man on his knees refilling the vending machine chips in with some folk memories of Juan. One of the ladies hazards a guess that Juan was some kind of warrior. She mimes a burst of sub-machine gun fire, shooting from the hip. The irony in this is that in 1936 General Franco sent his troops in to kill 200 wounded republicans in their beds in this very hospital. (Beevor).

Out in the narrow cobbled streets, I don't like finding that half the shops are devoted to selling souvenir swords and suits of armour, and I don't like being jostled and bossed about by tour guides leading swarms of tourists from all corners of the earth, and I don't like having to flatten myself against stone walls every other minute to let through a white van or a fat Mercedes. There are priests in black suits everywhere, with briefcases and cross faces. The arrogance of these clergy was why the king had already moved his court away to Madrid before Juan came here. (Boyd. 'the Companion Guide to Madrid and Central Spain'.)

To walk through Toledo is said to be to walk through the world, because there you will find people of all nations, provinces, professions, crafts, estates of life and languages (Christian). Its streets have been described as descending tunnels of darkness, cobbled, enclosed by massive walls of high stone, the sky above no more than a couple of fingers wide, the cheerfulness of lighted windows absent, massive doors studded with rusty nails, each one like the gate of a prison, the houses looking as if pretending to be asleep (Morton). During Juan's lifetime, the poet Garcilaso de la Vega described this place as 'a clear and illustrious nightmare'.

Church bells ring, not sweet bells or chiming bells, but deep-throated, rather angry catholic bells. I am summoned to the cathedral. But first I must buy an entrance ticket, obtainable only from a shop across the road. When Juan was held in Toledo he was, of course, never able to come to the cathedral, which at that time employed 524 ecclesiastics (Martz). My own link to the cathedral is through the Book of Common Prayer and the opening prayer of evensong, 'Dearly beloved brethren, the Scripture moveth us in sundry places to acknowledge and confess our manifold sins and wickedness ...'. This was originally a prayer developed in Toledo for their own use by the Mozárabes, Christians living under Muslim rule. When Cranmer was drawing up his Prayerbook, one of his eclectic helpers came upon this prayer and Cranmer liked it enough to include it (Morton).

I find the cathedral to be hugely gothic and elaborate but hardly worshipper-friendly. Facing the gigantic altar set-up is a small space, presumably for those few parishioners who matter. Then the whole nave is blocked by a huge cage containing the choir and organ. The back end of this is solid stone and floridly carved. This is all that the ordinary parishioners, whose place is behind the choir, at the back of the cathedral, can see while mass is being celebrated beyond it at the distant east end.

In October 1577, Juan was sufficiently recovered in the hospital to be able to travel, although still physically very run down. Mendoza, the hospital administrator, felt that it was time for Juan to leave Toledo. He provided him with two of his own servants to accompany him and mounted him on a donkey. They left town by the gate closest to the hospital and straightway crossed the river by the Alcántara bridge, which was built by the Moors in 997AD on Roman foundations and still stands today. Cántara means a churn in modern Spanish. Kantara, arabic for a crossing place, seems more likely. They turned southwards and started a long trek of some 165 kms, 30 leagues across La Mancha, bare and dusty all the way, and somewhat empty, as it still is.

I shrink from its emptiness, its 30 hours of walking, five days for me without benefit of much hospitality. Not having a donkey to get on I swallow my pride and get on a bus across the longer stretches for some of the way.

# 11   SAFE, OUT OF SIGHT

Safe, out of sight, unseen, on the move, Juan on his donkey was temporarily nowhere, as I am on my bus.

Around me slump pale students of Toledo's university.  I think they are sleeping off the effects of their Friday night and heading home to their families for the weekend.

The road rises from the Tagus valley that loops around the oppressive city.  It heads up past clumps of evergreen oaks, in places now cleared for olive groves.

Piesma, Orgaz, Yébenes, Guadalerza, Darazután, Zarzuela (meaning both a light musical drama and a seafood stew), Malagón, Peralvillo and Ciudad Real.  These are lovely words.  When Juan passed this way there were wayside inns never more than three to five leagues walk apart.  In my first 18 leagues, 100kms in the petrol age, I see just two such possibilities.  The first is a hostal which looks open and thriving.  The second is a run-down bar with the word camas, beds, painted crudely on the wall.  But the paint is peeling and the door is chained and padlocked.

After the hills, there are flat, burnt stretches and seams of red earth.  The watercourses are dry.  There is a hot sun through thin low cloud above the vastness.  Where the land is cultivated it seems to be well tended.  But no one is at work and there is very little sign of habitation.  Every five leagues or so a range of hills pushes up out of the plains.  Whenever Don Quixote and Sancho Panza travelled through New Castile across La Mancha it was through deserted and rugged landscapes like these, unfenced and unhedged as they have always been.  'They left that place and travelled all that day and the next without meeting anything worth notice, 'til they came to the inn which was so frightful a sight'.

Juan had plenty of time to think over his recent experiences and his faith.  Faith is a dark night to the soul, he would write in his 'Ascent of Mount Carmel'.  After nada of the senses and nada of the spirit he could achieve nada of faith.  This was how he explained it.  Having put to rest the senses, depriving oneself of all desire for worldly things, and having put to rest the spirit, through detachment from all spiritual imaginings, the soul can lean on pure faith alone in its journey to God.  And pure faith alone is darkness without light of understanding, and it leaves behind all natural reasonings and spiritual fancies. Faith is as dark as night to the understanding. Don't think about it. Don't try to make sense of it. It can be compared to midnight, which is total darkness. It is a gift by which God allows us to go beyond reason into the reality of the divine. It is escape in the dark to God. Juan wrote a beautiful poem about this. It was a poem of escape by night like his own recent escape, and it was a love poem, since, for Juan, to find God was to find love. He called it, 'Songs of the soul that is joyful to have reached the high state of perfection, which is union with God, by the path of spiritual negation'. Juan's loving soul, of course, was feminine to God's masculine, be that in Father, Son or Holy Ghost form. And their mystical union was beyond human sensibility. Mind, body, senses, spirit, these were stilled, as 'my house all quiet above'.

> On a dark night,
> I am burning with longings to love,
> Chance of delight!
> Unseen, on the move,
> With my house all quiet above.
>
> Safe, out of sight,
> By the secret hidden stair,
> Chance of delight! And my traces nowhere,
> With the house all quiet up there.
>
> In this night of loving,
> In this secret on which no-one spied,
> I seeing nothing,
> With no light or guide,
> But my heart's eagerness inside.
>
> And that will direct me,
> More certain than daylight can show,
> To where He will expect me,
> Whom I well know,
> In the union where none else is so.

Night you find me,
More fondly than the dawning sun:
Night you bind me
Lover with loved one,
Beloved into the lover spun!

Such flowers in my breast,
Just for him kept intact and alive,
So still there and at rest,
I will treat him to receive,
Breath of cedars the air I will breathe.

From the ramparts the air,
When his hair I ruffled and woke,
His hand cool and clear,
On my neck a stroke,
All my senses suspended in shock.

Rest there, and forget,
Brow on the Loved One reclined,
All ceased and quit,
My cares resigned
Among lilies and out of mind.

In translation, I have kept, again, the rhyme scheme, the number of stresses per line, and each image and thought in its original line in order to maintain the order of Juan's thought process.

The road passes an ancient, four-square fortress set on a hill top about half a kilometre away. A good position – you can command the road when you need to, but you don't want to have every weary wayfarer leaning on your door. It is abandoned.

The further south I go the more widespread are the olive trees.

I leave the bus and take to my feet again after the sprawling, modern city of Ciudad Real, Royal City, capital of La Mancha. Many of the early colonisers of Latin America in Juan's time were from these parts, fortune hunters from this poor hinterland.

The Castile that Juan was born into had been shaken to its foundations by Columbus's shocking discovery of another continent beyond the ocean (Petrie, 'Philip ll of Spain'). In 1552 a Spanish writer claimed that, 'The greatest event in the world since its creation, except the incarnation and death of the creator, has been the discovery of the Indies, and that's why they are called the new world' (Pérez). The conquest of the Americas was a prolongation of the Castilians' earlier reconquest of Spain, with a Bible in one hand and a sword in the other, an imperial mission for God. And for gold.

Each soldier of conquest was rewarded with about a hundredweight of gold and silver, a quantity which a man could barely lift (Lalaguna, 'A traveller's history of Spain'). During Juan's lifetime more than 160 million ducats worth of treasure was brought from the new world into Spain. Inflation rose with the volume of precious metal imports.

With treasure as an objective, it was an itinerant form of conquest and occupation. No more than 100,000 Spaniards crossed the Atlantic in the sixteenth century to explore some five million square kilometres. But, in Castile, the steady drain of men to exploit the Americas was compounded by the increased demand for cloth to sell to the Americas, which, in turn, drew people off the land into the towns. Large tracts of agriculture went out of cultivation (Hume). From the 1570s, rural Castile entered a period of acute and worsening distress (Lynch). Nevertheless, Spain now ruled much of the globe – large territories in Europe, the Americas, Africa, India and the Philippines (Kealey, 'Bacon's Shadow').

We are heading for a place called Almodóvar, Juan and I, but first we come to Puertollano. Puertollano means the flat pass and it does stand on a patch of flat ground, a gap between two hills. It is the last town before Andalusia and it has been a frontier town, once rich in mining for lead, manganese, copper pyrite, iron and coal. Now only one open-cast coal mine remains, and signposts to a petrolo-chemico complex.

From anywhere in town one can see pale surrounding crags with what appear to be steep sand drifts lodged high up in them. Down in the flat pass I am bombarded by large flies. When I sit down on a street bench, small moths take over and swarm into my face. Heavy, occasional rain drops fall. I buy a bottle of red wine which adds to my general air of vagrancy.  I ask the lady in the small shop for her most expensive bottle. It turns out to cost the equivalent of 50p and to be fit for purpose, harsh with the taste of mining and not to be swallowed without being noticed.

I am able to breakfast along with several teams of petanca players who are in town for a torneo.  And then I walk off towards Almodóvar del Campo. I re-enter the La Mancha of old.  To my right is the scorched plain and to my left a steep ridge of olive groves.  I have left the industrial revolution behind and come back to nature.

By the time Juan rode his donkey along this quiet road, he had already composed the first ten verses of his great work, 'The Spiritual Canticle, songs between the soul and the Bridegroom'.  It was a love story again, a search for loving, in which the soul, Juan's soul, is the feminine side of the relationship, the female partner, and God, the Christ, the Holy Spirit, the masculine side, the male partner.  The girl is searching for the boy in this poem.  The Spanish word for soul is, of course, feminine and the word for God masculine.  Juan's inspiration for the Spiritual Canticle was the Old Testament Song of Songs composed by Solomon.  Juan saw both the Song of Songs and his own Canticle as allegories on the quest of the soul for God and for mystical union with God, written in the language of a love affair which can be consummated only on the cross.  Both songs are saturated in the natural world.  Sometimes the metaphor for the Bridegroom is a stag, and for the Bride a dove.  The search is described in dialogue.  My usual rules of translation apply.

**BRIDE**
Where is your hiding place,
Loved One?  Left sighing, I say.
You're the hart in the chase,
And I'm wounded in the affray;
I clamour out after, but you're away.

Oh you shepherds who might be
On that hill for the sheepfolds over there,
If by chance you should see
Him I most desire,
Say I'm smitten and hurt to expire.

112

My searching is love struck,
By those crags will I go and by gulfs there,
No blooms will I pluck,
No beasts will I fear,
And I will pass fortress and frontier.

## QUESTION TO THE CREATURES

Oh forest and brush,
Planted by the hand of the Loved One!
Oh pastures lush
With flowers set on!
Tell me if past you he's gone.

## RESPONSE OF THE CREATURES

Scattering grace thousandways,
He went over these downs at a pace,
And going by with a gaze,
Just a glance from his face
Clothed them with beauty's trace.

## BRIDE

Oh thou who can heal!
End it in truth and give way,
Don't send what you will,
More go-betweens today,
Not knowing what I want them to say.

And those wayfarers who go,
Reporting your graces by the thousand,
All wounding me more so,
And leaving me moribund,
Their babble not for me to understand.

More, how to keep trying,
Oh my life not alive where you live,
Rendered so because dying
Of the arrows you receive
From the Loved One that, within, you conceive?

Why, since you have damaged
This heart, no healing give?
And since it is ravaged,
Why thus leave
And not take what you bereave?

Calm me of my fret
That no-one else is enough to undo,
And my eyes on you set,
Since their light you imbue,
And I need them only for you.

To be continued, when Juan, whose searching was love struck, had passed fortress and frontier.

As I walk into Almodóvar, I pass a small abandoned mining works and then a large cheese factory, still in business. Sheep's cheese. Reassuringly, a large flock of sheep, mainly white but with one or two black ones, straggles across the road. I hang back, not wanting to upset the sheepdog. A great cloud of dust crosses the road with the sheep and they move off across the stubble towards a small hill.

On the hill is an old white windmill, my first in La Mancha. There would have been hundreds for Juan to see, of course, on this trip. And for Don Quixote to tilt at. Cervantes tells us that Don Quixote intended to go to Almodóvar del Campo but was distracted from it by the appearance of a naked, lovelorn madman and by the theft of Sancho's ass. Looking more closely at my windmill, I see that there is a cast-iron Quixote on a cast-iron Rocinante tilting at it. Quixote is forever flitting in and out of his native landscape just as Cervantes himself flits in and out of his own created story, in different guises (Byron, 'Cervantes a Biography'). He is everywhere at once and nowhere, as God is.

I come into Almodóvar and search about this nice small town. When Juan came here there were 20 public inns. Now I am here I don't see any.

I am delighted to encounter a large concrete head of Juan. Only it looks nothing like him. It has a long, rectangular face and a great magisterial beard. And it has his name wrong, describing itself as San Juan de Ávila. There is more confusion for me when I come across another Juan statue, this time in bronze and calling itself San Juan Bautista de la Concepción. Who are all these San Juans? I find plaques recording the birthplaces of both these impostors but nothing about my Juan who spent two weeks here in the autumn of 1578.

A kind old man who has been watching me hovering about takes me in hand. He explains that Almodóvar is blessed by being the birth place of two saints, both named Juan, one before and the other after my Juan. He leads me to a small street once called Calle de San Diego, now Beato Juan Bautista de la Concepción. Here was the little monastery of the descalzos Carmelite friars that Juan came to. The building has been reconstructed and has incorporated some of the old walls. It is for sale. On the wall beside the front door is a plaque. It says, 'In this house was celebrated the Chapter of the Teresan Reform. Among the chapterites figured St John of the Cross'. One can look down the narrow street and still see out to the usual wide horizons of La Mancha.

At this door knocked Juan, and he was taken in. The chapter was a sort of emergency meeting of descalzos. Participating were Antonio, Pedro, Gregorio, Gabriel, Ambrosio and Francisco. They welcomed Juan and took great care of him. Young Pedro was responsible for nursing him and looked after him as if the little friar were his own father. Juan responded with affection and gratitude.

Why had Juan, on the run from calzos Carmelites, chosen to come to this marginal Castilian township? It was, at least, quite a long way from Toledo. Also, it was in exactly the opposite direction from Teresa and from his home territory of Medina del Campo, which the calzos might have expected him to head for. Perhaps he had been invited to the chapter. At any rate, once there, he took part in it.

The descalzos at the chapter had gathered to discuss what steps they could take on their own behalf against the alarming attitude of the dominant calzos. Their first resolution was to send a representative to Rome to ask for papal approval for separating their descalzo network from the calzos, as what would be called a province of its own within the Carmelite Order. Since this was a dangerously provocative move, Juan suggested that those who approved it should actually put their signatures to it. They all signed. Some would come to regret it.

It was Juan's kindly carer, Pedro, who became the chapter's messenger to Rome. Juan, despite his love for Pedro, said to him, 'You will go to Italy shoeless and will return in shoes'. He was right. In Rome Pedro was both pressed hard and flattered and, once back in Spain, he turned his back on the Reform.

Another important resolution in Almodóvar went even further. Having decided to ask to become a separate Carmelite province of their own, the descalzos, before even sending their request, went ahead and elected their own leader of that embryo province. Antonio was elected to the title of Provincial.

Finally the chapter appointed Juan to be Superior of the monastery at a place called El Calvario. This was a remote backwoods, establishment in the hills across the border in Andulusia. The descalzos thought Juan would be off the beaten track and well hidden up there.

While the chapter was still in session a descalzo padre arrived from Madrid to warn them that what they were doing would be seen as illegal within the Carmelite Order and that the papal authorities would be hostile.

They went ahead with it, all the same. Within a month the papal nuncio in Madrid had aborted their idea of a descalzo province, had placed all descalzos under the total jurisdiction of the calzos, had imprisoned their break-away Provincial, Antonio, and had issued a sentence of excommunication against Juan. This sentence excluded him from participating in any of the rites of the catholic church and, in particular, from the sacraments. The descalzos had put their principles into church politics and been broken for their pains.

Unaware that he had been cast out, Juan journeyed on by donkey in late October, southwards away from the calzo Carmelite power centres of Toledo and Madrid and towards his refuge in the hills. He was to leave his native Castile for the first time in his life to explore the doubtful pleasures of Andalusia.

# 12   OVER THE HILLS AND FAR AWAY, INTO ANDALUSIA

Off Juan went on his donkey to cross the burnt out southern end of the great, bare steppes of La Mancha. I know the route he took to his next place of refuge, 220 kilometres, 40 leagues away, so I follow him on foot, in good shape.

First we have to make our way back through the moths and the flies and raindrops of Puertollano. I glance up at a gigantic iron statue of a miner, a minero, staring from a vantage point above the town. Juan would have looked up at bare hillside here. No time to visit the Museum of Mining. It was October for Juan. It is June for me.

All along the first five kilometres of the flat valley bed that leads south-east out of town, the mines of Juan's day have been expanded into a vast, modern, industrial complex. This gleaming place is now a major source of energy – gas, coal, chemicals, and then a huge field of solar panels.

I am approached by a smartly dressed, young, black man, curious about where I am heading. I tell him about Juan. He is very courteous and, unexpectedly, he turns out to be English. He works here. When we part I hand over to him a paperback novel that I have just finished. I don't want to carry it any more but I don't like to throw a book away. I have found it to be, as he will find it to be, unexpectedly, a raunchy lesbian affair. Another man, seeing me to be a walker, promises me 40° of heat today.

Abruptly, the valley reverts to natural beauty and the traffic absents itself.

There are wild hills on either side. Even now, in June, the cuckoo and the hoopoe are still calling. The grass has already dried out, white, and there are a few bleached fields of oats. Occasional flocks of sheep move between scattered olive trees and evergreen oaks. In places, stretches of vivid brown earth, almost orange, are already ploughed, scarlet poppies flutter beside the gritty road, and bright yellow butterflies. I am drugged by the rhythm and the distance of my walk, rapturous, strong. This looks and feels, to me, like a holy land, like the Holy Land. And, beyond, vast space. I can see forever, here. Did Juan look up and wonder at it?

Hunched over his donkey, poor little Juan was still very much weakened by his torments in Toledo. He had been physically wrecked and was not yet restored. He was probably not of a mind to raise his head and to admire the landscape. Besides, he still saw it as a distraction. 'There is an important benefit in detaching oneself from created things: it leaves the heart free for God', he wrote in Ascent of Mount Carmel. And he would quote Jeremiah, 'I beheld the earth, and it was empty, and it was nothing; I beheld the heavens, and saw that they had no light'.

Oh, well, green signs inform me that I am, of course, on the Ruta de Don Quixote. None inform me that I am on the Ruta de San Juan de la Cruz, a real journey, not a storybook one. At least the signs are small and unobtrusive enough not to annoy.

I leave the valley through a pass that turns to the north-east. It is the Puerto de Calatrava, nearly 2,500 feet above sea level. Now on my left, high above the road is the Castillo de Calatrava la Nueva, the new. New, relatively, but built in the twelfth century. Once the threat of the Moors had ebbed away, it became home to a Sacro Convento. Perhaps Juan called in. There is a flag still flying above it, yellow, a banner with a strange device that I cannot make out. As I walk on, for miles and miles my glances back along the road are always dominated by this mighty fortress.

On a steep outcrop on the other side of the road stand the ruins of an even older establishment, now called the Castillo Salvatierra. It was built by the Moors around 1,000 AD to try and keep the Christians out of the foothills of the Sierra Morena, the brown range, the dark skinned, the Moorish, the great mountain rampart that protected the northern frontier of Andalusia and the Arab kingdom of Granada.

Once through this pass, this gateway, I am back in the proper landscape of La Mancha and the rolling plains stretch out ahead, endless and dusty.

And so to Calzada de Calatrava, which feels like a one-mule town. Calzada, they call it, which means roadway. This small place is simply here as a staging post on the road across the bottom end of La Mancha.

I check into a curious hospedería, a guesthouse, for the night. Set in a mean side-street, it is an ancient building of fine old brick that stands up proudly. It seems to be a small medieval fort. Inside, it is furnished with suits of armour, chivalric trappings, heraldic iconography, family relics. Beside my place at the great table in the baronial hall is a box of worn and clipped maravedies coins from Juan's time. Don Quixote would have loved this lodging. The old gentry whose home this once was have moved out into more practical accommodation nearby, so that they can let the rooms. I have the place to myself for the night.

The rest of the town has limped on into the 1940's. Old folk sit impassively outside their front doors. The various, advertised 'ermitas' are all inscrutably locked. The place feels introverted. People are small, like Juan of course. I wonder if Juan stopped here, 8 leagues out of Almodóvar, or whether his donkey trotted on.

My morning road soon rises again out of the plain into hilly country. It climbs more often than it dips. There are outcrops of rock, trees and bushes, with scorched grass between. There are many hurrying rabbits. There are partridges and an occasional harrier. On the road there are dead snakes and a dead buzzard. Its downy rib-cage is cleaned out, its wings are awry and its great talons at the end of long furry legs grasp at thin air.

If Juan noticed any of this at all he still dismissed it as a natural, material surface to attract man's natural, superficial eye, a surface to distract the soul's true eye from looking into the darkness of nada, where it might discover the deeper reality of God.

Don Quixote, following the discreet green signs that mark his Ruta, saw the great sweep of the natural world around him as an empty stage on which his own efforts might animate a much more real world of ideals – God, truth, love, fidelity, courage, service, justice. He saw it as a bare stage on which to intervene in favour of those ideals, just as he was one day compelled by them to intervene violently on the stage of a puppet show he was watching.

So today I think much about transcendence.

Don Quixote was intending to go to Viso del Marqués but turned aside. Viso stood on Juan's path too and he certainly rode through it. As I come through a pass at 3,000 feet I see the little grey town below me, just one league ahead.

Viso means something seen, a material appearance, something glimpsed on the surface. It is a beautiful place. In the square, its fine fifteenth century church must have attracted Juan into it as appropriate for prayer, despite the irrelevant stuffed crocodile that hung, and still hangs, on one wall.

And this same church sheltered Isabella's corpse during the stormy night of 10 to 11 December, 1504, on its way from Medina del Campo to its resting place in the royal crypt in Granada. Dead or alive, she is so often in front of me on my road.

Next day I am confronted by the gateway to Andalusia. This is a deep labyrinthine fissure through the otherwise almost impassable Sierra Morena. It is ragged and jagged and often sheer. Side channels tempt the traveller towards hopeless dead ends. The crags tear open the clouds above. When Juan's donkey brought him through here it was a passage infamous for its banditry. Teresa, heading south on her mission of reform, had once wandered about in these gorges for days, baffled and lost. It is a frightening prospect. It is known as the Desfiladero de Despeñaperros. The defile of the throwing down of the dogs. Perhaps it acquired this unpleasant name from the massacre of a defeated enemy after a battle on the heights above, now unrecorded in the histories.

Work on a road was not started until 200 years after Juan came through. Before that, no wheeled vehicle could attempt this narrow, stony gully. Now that road is an autovia which is open only to wheeled vehicles. Only to motor vehicles in fact. There is no way through for a walker. So I am obliged to take a lift.

After the Desfiladero de Despeñaperros, I am afoot again towards Juan's next staging post, La Peñuela, a small monastery on the southern slopes of the Sierra Morena. I am in Andalusia for the first time in my life, just as Juan was when he came here.

This was a lonely mountain-side for Juan but I find myself in what claims to be 'a jewel of rational urbanisation', a town called La Carolina. It was built in the nineteenth century, on a grid system, and populated with artisans and tradespeople from other Spanish domains and from Central Europe, who were paid to settle here. The aim was to civilise the badlands and it worked. The town feels slightly colonial in a hispano-american way.

At 2,000 feet it is airy, with Andalusia's highest peak, La Estrella, standing above. It seems a pleasant and successful environment. Juan has been named 'patron' of the ciudad, for want of any other history in the place, but nobody seems to know anything about him. Just another place in Spain where his name is called upon in vain while his record is erased.

Juan did not hang around here and nor do I. We shall both be back, towards the end of the journey.

On the road again, the morning air is cooler. This is Andalusia so this is hilly. I am finally out of endless, high, flat, uncompromising Castile, the Castile that produced El Cid, Isabella, Teresa, Juan, Cervantes and Luis de Leon. And I am into the Andalusia of what? Of flamenco and de Falla, of Manolete and Lorca.

Hill after hill, the road around each one reveals more ahead. Much is coloured dark green, the dark green of olive trees and the dark green of evergreen oaks. In the scorched grass between the trees countless rabbits run. The egrets flapping overhead seem incongruous up here, far from flat marshlands. The iron tip of my staff swings metronomically into the grit beside the road.

Finally I come down onto Vilches, with its factories. Vilches seems to exist only to produce olive oil. The town has not a scrap of pretension to gentility. Before bed I clamber up to visit the perched remains of a seventh century visigoth fort, badly knocked about by the coming of the Moors a century later. I am sure that Juan did not indulge himself in such sightseeing. And then, on television, I watch a young bullfighter named de Luis, Kevin de Luis.

And so the road goes on through Arquillos, Navas de San Juan (no relation) and Santisteban del Puerto, heading east. Most of the way there is a ridge of hills on my right and an open plain on my left. The landscape must have looked much the same to Juan as it looks to me, that is if he bothered to look at it at all. Cultivation of olive oil must be more organised and intensive now, and numbered in millions of trees.

In the small towns, men of about my own age hang about with walking sticks, always ready to help with directions and distances.

After Castillar de Santisteban the road winds up to a pass at nearly 2,500 feet and cuts through towards Sorihuela del Guadalimar. Here I can look south across hundreds of square miles of beauty, bounded by the distant mountains of the Sierra de Segura. There are eagles flying above me, or perhaps vultures. All is still and clear and fine. It is hard to think that Juan would not have paused here to look for the first time across the great terrain that was to be his home for the next few years. And it is hard to think that he would not have been struck and perhaps even moved, like me, by its beauty and its scale. Surely his conviction, ingrained in him on the harsh and empty meseta, that nature is nada, is nothing, must have felt at least a first small twinge of uncertainty here. Surely he could not look, like me, on this and still proclaim in all certainty with Jeremiah, 'I beheld the earth and it was empty, and it was nothing; I beheld the heavens, and saw that they had no light'. Surely the beauty of this material world of the senses must have resonated for Juan, however faintly, with intimations of the nature of the spiritual world beyond. It is hard not to infer that the scope of such material grace in the world might be, at least, to suggest a world of spiritual grace, or at least hint at it rather than hide it. How should we be put off its scent by such beauty?

I go down the slope towards Sorihuela to the sound of sheeps' bells.

Below Sorihuela a shallow valley descends to the banks of the river Guadalimar. When Juan came through that first time he didn't know that two years later he and his descalzos would be granted a small farm in this valley, called Santa Ana. They would use it as a retreat and a place of rest from work on their travels around the region. Juan sometimes spent as long as a week here. As Crisógono de Jesús said, 'There was quiet solitude, the gentle sound of running water, vast horizons full of light, the fragrance of rock roses, thyme and rosemary'. The holding was on the right bank of the valley. I walk down it considering candidate buildings, few and far between, small and some derelict. Of course, Santa Ana is not identified. Perhaps it has been bull-dozed out of sight in the normal way. But I can look south at the vast horizons full of light. I find them soothing, as I know Juan did too. A joy for ever.

I cross the Guadalimar by an old stone bridge. But not old enough for Juan. He used to have to cross in a boat. The water flows green. The smaller rivers of Andalusia are not dried out by this stage of the summer as the smaller rivers of the meseta are.

Now it is all uphill for the whole afternoon, at slightly less than one league per hour until I reach the top of the extraordinary, perfectly conical hill on which the Moorish settlement of Iznatoraf sits like a crown of stone, at nearly 3,500 feet. Not much bull-dozing seems to have been done over the years in this ancient, isolated spot.

When Juan came to Iznatoraf a possessed person was brought to him. The man was tormented by evil spirits and when he saw Juan he cried out, 'Now we have another Basil on earth who will persecute us'. But Juan was able to work the possession out of him and leave him cured.

I scramble from Iznatoraf in the dust, down the steep and lonely camino that winds through bushes and olive trees, grateful for my staff to keep my footing. It feels like bandit country, a long way from home. Sure enough, three feral youths are in the way. None of them moves. Their faces watch me approach, expressionless, all humanity blanked out. They might just as well be looking at a lizard or a toad as at me. I edge past without risking setting them off with a smile or a greeting, and stagger on, sweating. Just as with the bulls on the path at Duruelo, I do not look back.

Coming into the scruffy town of Villanueva del Arzobispo – the archbishop in question is the tentacular Toledo one, of course – I am approached by a mild and churchy middle-aged man who takes me into the church of San Andrés and introduces me to the priest. This young man simply pushes some pamphlets into my hand, for he is under pressure. He is about to give a guided tour to six tiny old nuns. My mild and churchy friend advises me that I shall not find anything that I may be looking for at El Calvario and that I should head on instead to El Sanctuario de Nuestra Señora de la Fuensanta which is nearby. Next moment I am out on the pavement hearing the key turn in the lock of the church door as the young priest and the middle-aged mild man shut themselves in to do something private with the six tiny old nuns.

Where I stay, there is a noisy first communion party. Lunch for 140 family and friends ends at 10.00pm. These Andalusian young women's outfits look as if they have been designed and coloured in by sexually precocious infants.

Next morning I am up in the Sanctuario de la Fuensanta. Juan used to stay here overnight from time to time. It was built as a front-line Christian fortress. When the Moorish threat went away it turned itself into a monastery. By the time Juan arrived the Carmelite Order was installed. Later Juan would introduce some descalzos.

I sit in the fortress's great hall, which in our times, Juan's and mine, does duty as a church. I find it a difficult environment, fussy. It is prettified all over with statues, images, colourful hangings, electric candles, glitter, plaster and paint. The only things to look at that have not been messed about and have probably not changed since Juan looked at them are the rough stone columns that hold up the roof. I feel the need for nada in this place, the need to blank out all the glitz, to switch off the electricity, to cover the whole with the darkness and obscurity that Juan recommended. Two ladies walk around in the church, chatting and touching objects, statues, altar-cloths, images, ornaments in a seemingly ritualistic order – each has her own system. One of them, as she leaves, plants a loud kiss in the palm of her hand and blows it towards the virgin in her shrine. This all looks like superstition to me, as I think it would have looked to Juan.

Today our road comes down at last to our destination, Beas de Segura, passing two rival olive oil factories on the outskirts. One is branded San Juan de la Cruz. The other one is branded Santa Teresa de Jesús. The town itself feels rather off the beaten track in its valley. It is set principally along the west bank of its own little river Beas, still flowing well in high summer, whitewashed houses, grilled windows, pots of flowering plants, narrow streets. Its traffic flow is organised on the miniature maze system, for minimum fluidity.

Juan's donkey brought him, exhausted, into the centre of this small Andalusian town, and to the convent of descalza Carmelite sisters, tucked away just behind the parish church. It was late 1577. He knocked, and the nuns brought their prioress to look out through the iron grille of the parlour at the visitor. She knew him. She was Madre Ana de Jesús, the beautiful and intelligent young woman who had called in at Juan's second priory, Mancera, close to Duruelo, seven years earlier. She and Juan had made such a good impression on each other then that their mutual attraction would be lifelong. She saw him now shrunken, discoloured, bloodless, bent, trembling and mute.

Ana's first remedy for Juan was song. She stationed two young nuns with sweet voices in a cell close by to sing gently of suffering and love, '... or suffering is the dress of love.' So Juan's first cure was tears. Silent and still, he clung to the parlour grating to weep. Quietly the tears kept coming, streaking Juan's drawn cheeks, for his first hour among the descalzas of Beas. He was 35 years old, over the hills and far away, but this was as close to a homecoming as he ever experienced.

# 13   CALVARIO, THE QUIET WATERS BY

Juan's first few days in the convent in Beas were spent in quiet recovery. When he felt well enough he began to spend time in the parlour, talking with the charming Madre, Ana de Jesús. At first Juan did not have much to say but Ana did not hold back. When Juan did start to contribute he said something that surprised Ana into silence. He said of the great Teresa that she was 'very much his daughter.' Ana went off and wrote to Teresa that although Juan seemed very good he was too young to presume to speak of the Foundress as 'my daughter'. She said as much, too, to her nuns.

Later Ana would receive a reply from Teresa: 'Fray Juan de la Cruz is indeed the father of my soul, and one of those whom it does me most good to have dealings with, I hope you and your daughters will talk to him with the utmost frankness, for I assure you, you can talk to him as you would to me, and you and they will find great satisfaction, for he is very spiritual and of great experience and learning'.

Young Ana and her daughters were by then, indeed, finding great satisfaction in Juan. The first nun to come to confession wrote, 'My inmost soul was filled with a great light which brought quiet and peace'. To open one's heart to such a one as this, how wonderful. Ana and the others were soon sharing this experience. A special bond of love grew up between Juan and this little community of descalza sisters. Ana and her daughters would always be most dear to Juan's heart. But soon he had to leave them to take up his post as prior of El Calvario.

When I find the church and the little old Beas convent tucked away behind it, Juan is long gone and all, of course, is locked and silent. But there is a telephone number on the church door. I wander off. The river is full of rippling weeds. Tiny, hunched, lop-sided men hobble towards park benches, little clouds of tobacco smoke supported by sticks. The younger Andalusian men give me a negative glance, with some suspicion. The younger women, however, give one a fine look, positive and optimistic. And they seem to grow into jolly and robust old girls.

At last I pluck up the courage to call the telephone number that I have noted from the church door. A man answers and says that he can take me into the convent and its church if I can be there in just five minutes. I am a kilometre away so I have to run it and I cut a strange, gasping, sweating figure of an Englishman being shown into the convent. The man lets me look at a chasuble worn by Juan and a chair sat on by Juan. Also a beautifully hand-written document. I nod and pant but I can't make out which is Juan's signature.

The convento had 30 nuns in Juan's time. Now it has only 14, scraped together from Poland, Mexico and the like. The minimum is 15 so this place is living on a knife-edge. Through the revolving cupboard, we speak with the Madre, Ana's successor, without seeing her of course. I explain myself as best I can. I put a 20 euro note into the turntable, as a gift to the convent. Round it goes and out comes a little booklet about Juan and Teresa in Beas. But my 20 euro note has just got round to the other side and a shrill voice calls out to me to wait. The cupboard revolves again and this time I get a heavy book, 'Beas y santa Teresa' by P Efrén J M Montalva. Not the best of additions to a back-pack, particularly for a walker more interested in Juan than Teresa.

And walk I must, now, to El Calvario. It has come to assume for me a similar importance to that of El Dorado for the sixteenth century adventurers in the Americas. For me it is the place where Juan was so happy again, after his first bliss in Duruelo, way back on the meseta.

I start by asking a group of old men about how to find it, and what is the best route over the hills. They all agree that it is not possible. It is very steep. It is very complicado. It would be a 30 kilometre return trip. I would be lost. Next I ask two old ladies. They point the way straight up a steep alley called Calle de la Cruz. Then just keep going. Not complicado. 8 kilometres each way.

On a brilliant day of blue sky and bright colours I head out of town up the steep alley. Up flights of steps and then on and up stony tracks, zigzagging through hillsides of pine trees, all very beautiful and silent. Buzzards circle above but their mewing is off my auditory scale, muffled as it has been by the years. I pass the rock which Juan used to rest on when, coming over from El Calvario to visit Beas, he caught his first sight of his beloved convent below. I sit on it, too, for luck. I start to worry about the huge dog that once threatened Juan on this path. He was able to take all the anger out of it but that is not a gift that I have.

I go up some 8 kilometres. The path is often hard going, demanding big efforts and demanding difficult choices where ways diverge. Finally I am above the tree-line and on the bare ridge, at 3,500 feet, that separates the mountain's east side and Beas from its west side and El Calvario. The view is now of much fiercer, craggier peaks and of a much steeper, immediate descent. There has been no-one to be seen on the way up and there will be no-one to be seen on the way down.

The paths are even drier and stonier on this side and when I come into trees they are olives, not pines. It is harder work going down these paths than it was going up. And I have to concentrate my mind more carefully on my footing. Further down, the hillside has been taken over by intensive olive oil culture. Where the slopes allow it the trees are planted in lines. The ground consists of grit and loose stones with occasional boulders humping out of the dust. No grass. The seasonal watercourses are dead and dry too.

What I know about the site of El Calvario is that it lies barely a kilometre above the Guadalquivir river. And that four hundred years ago it consisted of a rented house and a small oratory, a cultivated kitchen garden, fig, orange, plum and cherry trees, a well and a spring. There was an abundance of fish and game. All around were pines, oaks, elms and rosemary. Forty years ago it was still a piece of flatter ground on the hillside, a couple of whitewashed buildings, some elm trees shading a well, and, all around, pine trees and aromatic shrubs (Brenan). On these bone-dry slopes, finding the well and the ever-flowing spring will be the key to finding El Calvario.

Seeing nothing of a well and a spring I eventually come down onto the narrow road that runs at the bottom of the valley close by the Guadalquivir. Walking along the road I come to a plaque set into a rock. 'In this place of the hermitage and convent of El Calvario lived San Juan de la Cruz in the years of 1578 and 1579.' At this point a tiny stream trickles out of thick undergrowth to go under the road towards the river. Is it the stream that rises at El Calvario? I circle back up the hillside a little way until I can see that this stream comes from a long way up the mountain, much more than a kilometre above the Guadalquivir river, and that it runs all the way down in a deep and overgrown gorge with no sign of a flatter piece of ground for Juan's little priory. Wrong stream.

I carry on coursing about on stony paths among the regimented olive trees, and suddenly it is right under my nose. A piece of flatter ground with a big, green, weedy patch in the middle of it. I investigate the weedy patch and find clear water trickling through it. I follow that up and find where the fuente gurgles out from among the stones. And nearby a patch of reeds conceals a huge hole in the ground, ripped open and much enlarged by mechanical diggers. This was the well. A great black rubber tube, as thick as my waist, emerges from the water at the bottom of the hole to writhe away out of sight among the olive trees. No oratory any more, no hired house, no vegetable garden, no fig, no orange, no plum and no cherry trees, no elms, no pines, no aromatic shrubs. Just weeds across the spring and a great irrigation hole in place of the brothers' well. Bulldozers and diggers have improved the heritage site the better to serve agri-business.

So I have found El Calvario, just a weedy patch on the side of a dry mountainside that now exists only to produce olive oil. An empty place, unpeopled, deconstructed, demystified, neglected. Just a damp little hollow to stick a great rubber tube into. I am glad to have found El Calvario but sad that it has not been cherished. It has been violated.

I shall cherish it in my mind. I shall stay with it as it was when Juan was here, as it was when it was fit to welcome him as the new Superior.

There were thirty friars practising a life of penance here, a life of fasting and praying, hardship and hair shirts. Juan was not going to do away with all their practices of penance, but the Juan who had survived Toledo and come to himself again in Beas was going to moderate the severity of his new brothers' way of life, and he was going to develop around them a spirit of faith, love and confidence which they had not previously known.

It would still be a very simple life. They slept on woven mats of rosemary and vineshoots. The main meal often consisted of crumbs of bread in Andalusian style with a bowl of broth made from wild herbs. Collecting the herbs, they would go out with their donkey and gather those that he ate and leave those that he avoided. On feast-days some spoonfuls of chick peas and a little oil were added to the herbs. One day when the bell was rung for dinner there was only one tiny crust of bread left. Juan blessed it and exhorted the brothers to bear their poverty with joy in imitation of Christ. They retired to their cells to do just that. Two hours later a letter arrived saying that bread, flour and provisions were on their way from a rich lady well-wisher in Úbeda. The friars of El Calvario considered this an act of God, 'the miracle of our father, Fray Juan de la Cruz'. Juan himself was not enthusiastic about the idea of miracles, the idea of God picking and choosing on whose account to intervene, the idea of signs from God being necessary to bring men to believe.

Juan led his brothers in prayer and in their outdoor work. And he taught them just as he had taught the nuns in Beas. 'He who works for God through pure love, not only does it not matter to him that men should know it, but he does not even do it that God should know it.' And even if neither God nor man should ever know it, he would not fail to render the same services and with the same joy and love. 'Have a general desire of imitating Jesus Christ in all his works, in conformity with his life, about which we must think in order to know how to imitate it and behave in all things as he would have done'.

In spite of Juan's gentleness, he did not fail to correct laxity that might lead to mistaken thoughts or actions. Often his corrections were not severe but designed to surprise the person concerned into thinking through their error – for example by withholding something that was too much taken for granted, however small.

Every Saturday Juan walked back over the mountain to Beas and the little convent where Ana de Jesús presided. On Saturday and Sunday he would confess the nuns and then talk with them. Sometimes he read with them a book of devotion. He was never in a hurry. A nun asked him why the frogs that were around a pool of water in the garden, almost before they could hear the sound of her footsteps approaching, leapt into the water and hid in its depths. 'That is what you must do,' Juan replied, 'Flee from creatures and plunge into the depth and centre, which is God, hiding yourself in him'. There, in the depth and centre, she, like the frogs in the pool, would be secure. He asked another, 'In what does prayer consist?' She said, 'In looking at the beauty of God and rejoicing that he has it.' This delighted Juan.

In Calvario, Juan would spend much time with his friars out in the natural beauty of the open country side. No longer, with Jeremiah, was he saying, 'I beheld the earth and it was empty'. In moving from the harshness of the meseta to the sweetness of Andalusia, Juan had been moving from condemning nature to treasuring it. Sometimes the friars went out to pray together among the wild flowers and in the woods, sometimes just to enjoy the natural world. Sometimes they worked together in the garden and the fields. Juan would speak to them of the marvels of creation which were before their very eyes in all their splendour, of the divine beauty in the very flowers at their feet, in the crystal clear waters that flowed and cleansed, of the birds singing in the trees, of the brightness of the sunlight. Juan wanted the friars to take pleasure in all this, as he now did.

Don't turn your back on life, Juan was telling them. Nature and people are in God. See them as God sees them (McGreal, 'John of the Cross'). If you can see them as God sees them they will be to you as signposts towards God. Juan wrote: 'Such things of the senses serve the end for which God created and gave them: that he should be better loved and known because of them'. Nature was a surface which might lead one into the mystery of God beyond. So we must look at the surface and try to see beyond it.

The reality of the forest was all that deep, living darkness, which one could not actually see, when one was looking at the forest's surface which was all that one could actually see – the nearest belt of trees (Ortega y Gasset, 'Meditations on Quixote'). But we needed to open something more than our eyes to make this deeper world exist for us. Thus a man of faith could see God in the flowery fields. And Don Quixote could interpret the signs of the natural world as signs that provided glimpses of a possible spiritual glory (Unamuno, 'Essays and Soliloquies'). 'How blind must he be that cannot see through a sieve,' said the Don.

Seen like this, the material world became spiritual, the physical universe nothing but clots of matter entirely neutral in themselves, whose qualities were wholly the quality of the spirit that inhabited them (Gorer, 'Africa Dances'). 'Do you think you see it all with your poor eyes? Do you see the wind, you who are so strong? You are just not able to look at a tree and see any other thing than a tree. You think that it is just emptiness, the air? The hill a hill and nothing more? The hill, you will make out what it is one day, the hill.' Thus an old seer dying in the hills to his hidebound son-in-law (Giono, 'Colline').

In 2009 the £1m Templeton Foundation Prize was awarded to a physicist whose research in quantum physics had led him to propose, as Juan had done before him, 'The possibility that the things we observe, our empirical reality, may be tentatively interpreted as signs providing us with some perhaps not entirely misleading glimpses of a higher reality'. He called it 'a mysterious, non-conceptualisable ultimate reality, not embedded in space and (presumably) not in time either' (d'Espagnet, 'On Physics and Philosophy').

For Juan, these things observed, these trees and hills, these clots of matter, these flowery fields, these things of the senses, these surfaces, this sieve, were there to draw us to look through them, to draw us towards heaven, towards that higher reality. And that higher reality was as close around us as the air we breathe. Only most of us, most of the time, walked through it like blind men.

It was glimpses of that higher reality that Juan was looking for when he looked at, looked into, looked through the natural beauty of El Calvario. It was Juan's hope that human beings, as fragments of the empirical reality of the created world could achieve meaning in life in being absorbed through the veil, the sieve, into the higher reality that was the creator's all-inclusive, mystical body (Dombrowski, 'St John of the Cross. An Appreciation').

Juan warned against trying to conceptualise that mystical body, that higher reality. 'Created things, whether earthly or heavenly, have no comparison to God's being. For God falls within no genus or species whereas created things do'. Juan would have agreed with Unamuno, who said, 'To seek to define God is to claim to limit him in our mind...In so far as we attempt to define him, we are confronted by nothingness'. As Antonio Machado put it, 'Oh gran saber del cero! Oh great wisdom of the zero!' And Karen Armstrong, 'We can say nothing about God'. Me too, I presume to know nothing, nada, up here in God's own country. But I come back in transcendent mood from El Calvario.

Juan found conditions in his lovely convento encouraged him to continue composing his mystical narrative poem. 'Spiritual Canticle'. It was the story of the quest by the soul, the dove, suffering from love, for the Loved One, the stag, God in Jesus Christ. The story of the girl searching for the boy, the Bride for the Bridegroom. The first ten verses had been created on the road to Almodóvar. The next twenty-one in El Calvario, and much shaped by his environment there. It is still a canticle of longing. It too is transcendent and it is mystical.

> BRIDE
> Your presence make plain,
> And kill me with sight of your brilliance;
> See how the pain
> Of love has no remittance
> Except by your presence and countenance.
>
> Oh crystal current,
> If only your silvery guise
> Would form in a moment
> Those longed for eyes,
> That my heart's designs devise!
>
> Look away with them, Loved One,
> For my flight is begun.
>
> BRIDEGROOM
> My dove, turn around,
> For the stag they would smite
> Appears on the high ground,
> Refreshed in the air of your flight.
>
> BRIDE
> Oh my Loved One, the highlands,
> The valleys of solitude tree-high,
> The strangeness of the islands,
> The torrent's outcry,
> The breeze a lover's sigh.
>
> The night so pacific,
> To the risings of dawn the prelude,
> The silent music,
> The resounding solitude,
> The bread of renewal love's food.

Bouquets make our bed,
With caves of lions all around,
And with purple spread,
In peace well-found,
By a thousand shields gold-crowned.

Tracking your traces,
Girls draw down the path for a sign,
For lightning strike places,
For zest in the wine,
Emanations of physic divine.

In the vault deep inside
I drank of my Beloved, and went out
Valley wide,
To things not known about,
And the flocks I was once with now without.

His breast there he gave me,
There knowledge deliciously professed,
And I gave him the whole tally
Of mine, nothing missed;
And there for his bride I made tryst.

My soul put to work hard,
And my output all in his service;
Now no livestock I guard,
Nor hold other office;
Now loving is my only exercise.

Since now like an outcast,
From today no more found or seen,
I'm given out as lost;
Loving on the run,
Myself I have lost and been won.

With blossom and emerald,
In morning's freshness sought,
We shall be girdled,
And love in you shoot,
And by a hair of mine be caught.

To that single hair
On my neck taking flight you attend.
You look on my neck there,
Find duress without end,
And, in my eye, yourself you rend.

When it is I whom you see,
Your eyes imprint me with your grace:
Your loving is for me,
And for merit repays
My own adoring gaze.

You'll wish me no scorn
If darkly discoloured you find me,
But well me discern,
And thereafter attend me
For the grace and beauty you lend me.

Catch the foxes that prey
On us here among flowers of the vine,
So with roses we may
Make all entwine,
And no-one come upon us down the incline.

Drop cold wind of death;
Come, south wind, loves to reacquaint,
Through my garden with a breath,
And stir the scent
Of flowers for the Loved One's nourishment.

BRIDEGROOM
The Bride is now present
In the sweet garden for which she so pined,
At rest and content,
Her neck reclined
Where the arms of the Loved One are kind.

Beneath the apple tree,
There with me you were wed,
Had my hand from me,
And were made good,
Where your mother, defiled, had stood.

This is the crux of it. Christ and the cross, the soul sharing Christ's cross in love, mankind redeemed and the defiled human race, Eve, once cast out of Eden from beneath the tree, restored beneath the cross and made good. Cut to El Calvario, and goodnight.

Now birds' lightness in the glide,
Lions, leaping bucks, fallow deer,
Hill and dale, riverside,
Waters, warmth in the air,
And watches of the night in fear,

With pleasant lyres,
And syrens songs I call
You to cease your ires
And not touch on the wall,
So the Bride safe asleep may fall.

Juan's lyrical interlude at El Calvario was soon over. His reputation had travelled 11 leagues, 60 kilometres, south-west to the university town of Baeza. The Doctors of the university were demanding insistently that he come and found the first college of descalzo friars in Andalusia. The Carmelite Order and the bishop of Jaen authorised the move. The prioress of Beas, Ana de Jesús, wrote a letter of recommendation. So in the spring of 1579 Juan came house-hunting, for a town-house in which to install his new college.

Farewell to the beauties of nature and then two days walk along the busy highway that runs from Albacete, on the Mediterranean coast, across to Cordoba and on down to the plains of Seville. Between El Calvario and Baeza much of it runs along a ridge of stupendous views, with the Guadalquivir river beyond all the olive trees below it to the left. Passing the Santuario de Nuestra Señora de la Fuensanta, I set out in earnest for Villacarrillo (a town called cheek-as in face), Torreperogil, Úbeda and Baeza.

At lunch on the second day, an armed man sits by my left elbow, pistol and holster, baton, radio, police badge and just a half bottle of red wine. On the last leg it proves difficult to get out of Úbeda on foot through the new autovia complex, like a hiker at Spaghetti Junction. At last I am on the good old road again and up into Baeza past its bullring.

# 14  HURLY BURLY IN BAEZA

I find Baeza to be a light and pleasant little town which seems to want to exploit its history but hasn't yet properly learnt the tricks of that trade. The ancient centre of tiny streets and alleyways can be enjoyed uncompromised by global tourism.  Here a few visitors just wander about vaguely.  The resident population is down to 15,000.

Baeza was a thriving centre of trade and culture, with a population of 50,000, when Juan walked in with the three friars who would comprise this new descalzo Carmelite foundation.  They took a house and, overnight, converted its largest room into an oratory with an altar, and its smaller rooms into cells for the friars.  They hung a bell from a window and rang it at dawn to share their excitement with their slumbering neighbourhood. The first mass they celebrated was on 14 June 1579, for the feast of The Holy Trinity.  Juan was coming up to his thirty-seventh birthday.

On the whole, the neighbours received them well.  They brought essentials, bedding and provisions, to help the priory of San José get started.

But the house itself did not receive them so well.  It enjoyed the reputation of being haunted.  It generated awful sounds in the night.  One of the young friars was so afraid that he had to move in with Juan.  In the darkness there was a great commotion of shattering crockery.  When daylight came there was no sign of any such breakages.  For a week the disturbance increased until, finally, it climaxed by throwing Juan and his candle to the floor as he came out of his cell.  This seemed to satisfy whatever it was because after this all was peace and quiet.

Next, novices from La Peñuela and El Calvario began to arrive.  Juan conducted both their spiritual and their academic education, at first limited to theology.  The foundation gradually took on the character of a college until it was recognised as such by the university under the expanded name of Nuestra Señora de Monte Carmelo y San José – giving it a more clearly Carmelite label.  In the new academic year, Juan was confirmed as rector of the college.  Juan's own students, and his teaching of them, became so much admired that many other students wanted to move in and take the descalzo habit.  Professors, too, used to turn up to seek Juan's guidance on obscure theological and scriptural issues. Despite himself, Juan was becoming famous in Baeza. When he ventured out into the streets he was followed about as a curiosity, even a celebrity.

So many people wanted to be involved that Juan opened up a series of public discussions on theological subjects in the college. The building had to be expanded. Students and professors crowded in. Juan chaired the proceedings, directed the debates and argued out and solved the difficulties that arose. He was now rarely alone and rarely at rest in this hectic town.

Nowhere in noisy Andalusia would Juan ever be as happy as he had been in his first quiet home in the province, at El Calvario. Perhaps, too, he was now missing Ana who had been just a short walk away over the beautiful mountain. In Baeza he found urban, Andalusian style at odds with his own. There was so much gossip, chatter and talent spotting. He wrote in his letters of not being able to endure these people, of being an exile, of having been swallowed by a whale and vomited up in a foreign port. He was, after all, a Castilian from the heart of Spain, and the frivolous Andalusians on the fringe seemed to him to be not typical Spaniards at all. Even English visitors can see the difference. They have noticed Castilians regarding the Andalusians as buffoons, without gravity or reserve (Pritchett). Or treating them with much the same affectionate tolerance that Englishmen [once] bestowed on the charming and inconsequential 'Paddy' (Morton). By preference the Andalusian lives wholly within his skin, his work inspired by laziness and aimed at achieving more laziness, wrote Castilian Ortega y Gasset.

More than three hundred years later, another poet and professor found himself just as ill at ease as Juan had been in Baeza. Antonio Machado taught French in the university for a few years and pined, in his loneliness, for Castile's pure silences. But in Machado's case, Baeza has done its best to keep his memory fresh. His classroom is preserved intact for tourists to gawp into. A new statue of him has been placed in a busy, pedestrianised street. There is even a college building named after him. Not for him the bulldozer treatment reserved for the great man Juan.

From the hurly burly of his life as rector, professor and prior, from all the words, the questions, the answers, the decisions, the attention, Juan sought calm in taking care of the humblest needs of his house. He washed, he swept, he cleaned latrines.

When Juan had been in Baeza for a year, the pope in Rome ordained that the austere, reformed, unshod descalzos were henceforth to be recognised as a separate Carmelite order in its own right. They were to be quite independent of the dominant, comfortable, unreformed, well shod Carmelite calzos. Juan would no longer be prey to the calzo thought police. But it would not be long before the descalzos themselves would be on his case.

In that same summer of 1580, a terrible epidemic swept across Spain. They called it catarro universal, and it was probably some form of Spanish 'flu. In Juan's home town of Medina del Campo his mother Catalina, now in her late sixties, went down with it. All the loving efforts of her eldest son, Francisco, could not save her. The descalzas, the Carmelite nuns of Teresa's foundation, up the street in Calle Santiago, took her body in, as the body of a holy person, and buried it in their own church. At the same time, Teresa herself was seriously ill with the catarro in the discalced convent in Valladolid. She recovered but it aged her.

When the catarro reached Baeza, all eighteen of Juan's living-in friars and novices thought they had caught it. Then nine more patients were carried in from El Calvario. Juan swung into action. He procured for them, and he himself prepared and served, finer dishes than they encountered in their everyday lives. His regime for the sick was to treat them with treats, to raise their spirits with stories and reflections, and to provide them with continuous quietly optimistic companionship. And if a medicine could provide a patient with the slightest perception of relief, even temporary, even merely psychological, despite the doctors' scepticism, Juan would somehow raise the money to buy it. 'God will provide', he would say. No-one in the Carmelite college died.

In the town hospital, outside the walls, extreme cases were being brought in from almost every family in Baeza, and some were dying there. Every day Juan hurried over to the hospital to help.

I follow him there, out through the Puerta de Úbeda, by which I have entered the town, and then south-west to cross an open space now called Plaza de España, and then I go fewer than 100 paces along a side street to the corner where the church of La Purísima Concepción still stands. Its adjoining hospital has gone, but the site is now occupied by a modern hotel and I can check in there for the night. This hotel is constructed to the same pattern as that of the demolished hospital, with a central courtyard and colonnades around. The whole modern hotel above rests on these original stone arches below. So I can walk across this central patio, as Juan walked across it, and pause to look up at the summer sky as he must surely have paused and looked. And rest against the same stone columns.

The big question I want to solve is this. Where have they hidden the house that contained the first little college which Juan presided over as rector? The search is not made easier by two name changes and one additional location. From San José it grew to become the expanded Nuestra Señora de Monte Carmelo y San José. Having first expanded within the city walls, it then needed to add premises without. On 3 March 1581 these new premises formally became the university's college of San Basilio, in Calle Carmen, 200 paces north of the Puerta de Úbeda. The site of this second building is easy to find. It is now occupied by a weed-infested basketball pitch and a forsaken looking statue of my man. Not a very good likeness.

But where was Juan's first house in Baeza, the priory of San José? As usual, I go to the tourist office. There are two girls, apparently students, behind the counter. I put the question to them. The older of the two is delighted to be able to mark the place for me on my map, in a short street called Calle Cruz. Her family have always known where it was because their house is actually on the very site of Juan's priory. This solution is no good to me because this girl's family home is far outside the old city walls to the west in an area that was probably not urbanised until some 200 years after Juan had left Baeza. In his day this was probably just a blasted heath. Disappointed, I am ungracious enough to point this out to the poor girl.

The Baeza Museo is closed for improvements for at least another year, and so is unable to help me.

Back at the hotel I explain my mission to the young man and the young woman behind the desk. The young man becomes interested in my idea of translating the sixteenth century Spanish of Juan's poetry. The problem he sees in it is that the Spanish language continued to shift and change until much later (not having a literary fixative to stabilise it as English, for example, had the King James Bible and Shakespeare). The young man gets carried away and seizes upon a meaning for a particularly difficult phrase of Juan's, in the Spiritual Canticle, that would make it a premonition of the phylloxera outbreak that devastated so many French and Spanish vineyards three centuries later.

Turning to the dark and pretty young woman, with her computer, I find her a great help in looking for the San José priory, particularly in tracking street name changes. Together with her, I choose my spot, and the more I go on to find out about it the more right I feel I am. I walk to the site and it feels right. I then bring to bear four further factors that seem to confirm it.

In a dark little bookshop I find a book about San Juan in Baeza written by the town's most energetic and prolific historian, Pedro Ayala Cañada. He has consulted manuscripts in the Biblioteca Nacional Madrid and he says that the house occupied by the San José priory was within the walls to the south-east of the Úbeda gate, next to what 'today belongs to the heirs of D José María de los Río, Calle Horno de la Merced No 1'. Horno means oven. Merced means a favour granted. This is, indeed, my chosen spot. I put my case to the lady of the bookshop, who seems to be of an academic bent. She telephones a real academic friend. They give their sanction to the little cross I have marked on my tourist map.

I come across a print of an old sketched view of the city entitled Vista Septentrional (northern) de la Ciudad de Baeza. It is in fact a view from the west. But correctly placed and labelled are the cathedral, the original university and the new one, the hospital, the city walls, and the Plaza Mayor ( now Paseo de la Constitución). And there are Juan's Carmelites just where I have put them, spot on.

This location would also have ensured that his route to the hospital went down in a south-westerly direction, near the great tower of Aliatares, as Crisógono has told us.

And, given that Juan was where I have put him, it would have made sense that, when he needed to expand to a second site outside the walls, he would have selected one in nearby Calle Carmen, where the basketball court now is.

The only trouble with my chosen spot is that it does not conform to some of the distances quoted by Crisógono, who has been the one person most informed about the life of Juan de la Cruz since Juan lived it himself, and died. Crisógono says that Juan was 500 paces from the Úbeda gate, whereas I make it 150 paces at most. The dark and pretty hotel girl tries to reassure me by saying that the length of people's paces might have been much shorter in olden times. Crisógono also says that Juan was not far from the university (at that time in the Baeza Museo building – the new university building did not open until 15 years later), whereas I have him about as far away from it as it is possible to get in Baeza – some 700 paces. But if he had been somewhere near the old university as Crisógono says he could not have walked south-west to the hospital. He would have had to walk due north.

I can only think that Crisógono has not criss-crossed the ground as much as I have, back and forth, counting paces and checking bearings.

I spend some time enjoying hanging around beside the site of Juan's house. The Calle Horno de Merced has at some time in the past pierced and blasted through the old city wall from the extramural, northern, side to extend as the Travisia (passageway) del Horno de la Merced into a small and attractive square inside the walls. No-one can tell me what this square is called. Someone suggests Plaza Antigua. From it there are fine views to the south, towards the mountains of the Sierra Almadén.

The bulldozers have finished with Juan's priory of San José, the first descalzo Carmelite university college in Andalusia. In its place stands an almost completed, small apartment block with electric cables sprouting from its concrete, waiting to be finished off. Workmen go in and out. It seems to be called El Mirador, the viewpoint. Or perhaps Balcones de Guadalquivir. It doesn't look bad, reasonably plain, not too mannered. All the apartments are still for sale, for we are in a recession. I wonder whether this building will set upon its new occupants with poltergeists as the old building did. I ask the foreman whether he knows that this was where Juan de la Cruz lived and worked. He nods. I ask him whether it wouldn't have been a good idea to name the building after Juan. He shrugs and smiles.

It is time to look for dinner. Every restaurant seems to be shut. I am eventually directed to a door beside a Franciscan convent. The vast, renaissance, stone hall is big enough to seat 500, but I dine alone. By my table, on a sort of sideboard, is a half-size plaster statue of St Teresa. Behind her on the wall hang nine pendulum clocks. The clocks have stopped. All the pendulums just hang down, quite still and silent.

Time never stood still for Juan. He was the heartbeat of Baeza and an object of fascination to its women. The city was buzzing with beatas and Juan's arrival generated more. These were women who, without abandoning the world to shut themselves away in a convent, adopted a daily life of penance and prayer as if they actually were nuns. Some of them formed pious groups and hurried about the streets in uniforms of matching habits. Some were wealthy and doled out largesse to the poor. A rich and beautiful girl called María, much fancied and sought after by the bachelors of Baeza, dressed herself in coarse cloths and, putting a great cross on her shoulders and carrying a sewing needle in her fingers, went out into the market crying, 'Long live the poverty of Jesus Christ!' After that she was never married.

Many women would crowd into Juan's little Carmelite church to confess. At their insistent request, he provided a group of them with a set of rules by which to live their lives. And later he allowed them to wear the descalzo habit. One of them, Teresa, reached such a high point in her life of prayer that she had frequent visions, revelations and raptures. She had a saintly reputation and acquired the nick-name, Madre Teresa.

Another María, a widow, was persecuted by the devil who threw her to the ground at the door of Juan's church. She was not only knocked unconscious by the force of her fall but was also so rooted to the ground by it that bystanders could not lift her body up. Juan was called to the door and María immediately stood up and walked away quite free of the devil. But on subsequent occasions the devil would throw her down again and now would free her only after Juan came out and gave her communion on the pavement where she was lying.

One of Juan's devoted penitents was Juana, who lived opposite and had been only fifteen years old when she had been woken by the bell on that first morning. She had helped clean the church for the first mass, and she became a beata for life.

Another María was only 16 and would confess to Juan three times a week, on Sundays, Tuesdays and Fridays, all the time that he remained in Baeza. Forty years later, this María would give evidence on oath, in the first enquiry in the long process that would eventually declare Juan a saint, that she had never heard an idle word from him or seen in him a gesture of imperfection.

Another Juana became rather more of a problem. She was a beata with a great reputation for sanctity. She was credited with miracles, revelations and raptures. She begged to be allowed to go and join the nuns in Beas as a lay-sister and this was eventually granted. Madre Ana de Jesús, the young prioress, sometimes found Juana's enthusiasm hard to take. She had to say to her, 'Sister, here we don't need your raptures, but that you should wash the dishes well'. Soon afterwards, strange noises in the night could be heard from Juana's cell. There was a shock in store for the nuns who opened her door. An unbearable stench blew out into their faces. Then, in the candlelight, they were embarrassed to make out Juana's naked form, writhing about on her back on her mattress in, as Crisógono puts it, 'an unbecoming posture'. Juana's explanation was that she was with Jesus Christ. She said that, from the time she was a child of seven, a very beautiful boy began to accompany her and grow up with her. By the time they were both thirteen they were married and living in the state of matrimony. As reward, Jesus Christ gave her visions and raptures. 'Sister, it is the devil who has deceived you', the Beas nuns told her. Even after being turned out of the convent, Juana carried on in her error. Eventually the Inquisition gave her a hundred lashes as she walked through the streets with a black candle in her hand. This auto de fe cured her. Juan looked back on this as a case where he was to blame for not having been aloof enough in his dealings with this woman. He had been too kind with Juana, he had insisted that she should be given the descalzo habit, and thus he was implicated in what had become a very serious sin.

In the turmoil of Baeza, the Lord's Prayer must have been a great stand-by to Juan. Forgive us our trespasses as we forgive them who trespass against us, lead us not into temptation, but deliver us from evil. Amen.

## 15 BYWAYS TO GRANADA

From his duties in the city of Baeza, Juan was frequently called to journey into the lovely valleys of the Guadalquivir, the Guadalimar and the Beas rivers to minister to Ana de Jesús and her nuns, to the friars of El Calvario and to the farm establishment of Santa Ana.

As he wandered along, almost always accompanied by one or two close companions, he would cheerfully sing hymns and recite psalms and his own mystical poems. Perhaps it was now that he adapted an ordinary pastoral love song of the day and added a last verse, turning it into a religious poem. Christ, unrequited in his love for our soul, was the young shepherd, abandoned and forgotten by his love, who hanged himself on a tree, stretched out his arms and died, crucified.

> A lonely shepherd lad forlorn,
> Far from ease and unresigned,
> Brought his shepherdess to mind,
> And his breast for love was torn.
>
> His tears for wounds of love were not.
> Nor for being beset by pain,
> Although to heart he took the bane,
> But tears to think he was forgot.
>
> Only to think he was forgotten
> By his shepherdess, so greatly hurt
> He went to exile treated like dirt,
> His breast with love so sorely smitten.
> The shepherd said; Unhappy luck
> In the one that turned my love to absence
> And not to want to enjoy my presence,
> And my breast with her love so sorely struck!
>
> And at length at the end himself he elevated
> Upon a tree his fine arms wide,
> And held by them there, stayed where he died,
> His breast with love so sorely penetrated.

'Let us not forget! Although we may be seeking God, the beloved is seeking us still more', wrote Juan in his Living Flame of Love commentary. And it was in the crucifixion that 'Christ accomplished the reconciliation and union with God of all mankind at that very moment when He was most annihilated in all things, brought lowest in the estimation of men' (Ascent of Mount Carmel commentary). 'This was the moment when our Lord was most reduced to nothing in everything. He was reduced to nothing with respect to human reputation, for when men saw him die they mocked him rather than esteemed him'. Juan saw that Christ deliberately took upon himself to experience the very worst of what it is to be human, to experience for himself the degrading failure of all justice, compassion, respect, life. Knowing this we could be sure that he now truly empathised with us, forgave us and loved us in our sinful, abusing, suffering and despairing human state – rather than despising us for it. He too had been there. By sharing it he redeemed us rather than condemned us.

> And as for their sin,
> From it he would rise,
> In manner such that no-one
> Would them now despise.
>
> Because in every semblance
> He would to them comply,
> And he would come among them,
> And among them he would die     (Romance 4)

'He who seeks not the cross of Christ seeks not the glory of Christ,' wrote Juan in his Sayings of Light and Love.

Juan was quite clear, however, that Jesus was not sent by God as a go-between. No, for Juan, God and Jesus were the same, from the beginning, they were aspects of one God for which we sometimes use different terms: Father, Son. Holy Spirit. So to hear the word of God from Jesus was simply to hear the voice of God.

> In the beginning abode
> The Word, and lived in God.
>
> The Word called itself Son
> Which was born from the beginning.

And thus the glory of the Son
In the Father did rest,
And all his glory the Father
In the Son possessed.

Like loved one in lover
One in other resided,
That love bound them together,
In that same they confided. (Romance 1)

'One word spoke the Father, that was his Son, and speaks that always in eternal silence, and in silence has to be heard by the soul', Sayings of Light and Love again. So Christ was God expressing himself in our world, from the higher reality of the other side.

To Juan, Christ was more than a message from heaven to earth, he was the touch of heaven on earth. 'God's greatness and glory are shown to us, by the touch of Jesus, with love and tenderness rather than with awe and terror'. 'What we experience in God's touch is in some way a foretaste of everlasting life'. (Living Flame of Love commentary). So God's touch, Jesus, was indeed God himself made flesh and blood. Here was God, for once and for all time, penetrating the veil that separates our created world from the higher reality that is God himself, and penetrating that veil in the form of flesh and blood. God as a man, Christ, to touch us. Juan's soul cried out in burning love for that touch.

Oh flame of love alive,
How tenderly you fret
My soul in its profoundest centre!
Since now not fugitive,
Complete now will you yet,
Break through the veil to sweet encounter.

So thank goodness for the little farm of Santa Ana below Sorihuela where Juan's spirit could sing like this, away from the bustle of Baeza. Walking through this place on my way to Beas, as Juan used to, I too feel the atmosphere of peace, silence and beauty, the quiet solitude, the gentle running water, vast horizons full of light (Crisógono's words).

And thank goodness for El Calvario, only a day's walk from the farm, then with its gardens and groves, chapel and well, all now sacrificed to the mercenary and voracious culture of olive oil.

Above all, thank goodness for Beas, for young Madre Ana and her sisters, partners for Juan in the ministering of his most intense and fruitful spiritual direction. Just a morning's walk over the mountain from El Calvario, Beas was once again cleansed of all error and a haven of love in God.

Juan was at Beas when an order came to him from the Vicar-Provincial of the newly independent descalzo Order of Carmelites in Spain. He was to take Madre Ana de Jesús from Beas to Granada and set her up there in a new foundation as prioress. This trip would turn out to bring to an abrupt end the Baeza chapter in Juan's life and to open a new Granada chapter.

The marching orders arrived on 13 January 1582. A terrible storm immediately broke out in the valley of the Beas river, with such fury that anyone who ventured outside felt that they were 'drowning in water and stones', as Ana put it. And a sudden illness came upon her, so severe that the doctors were frightened. But nothing could stop these unshod Carmelites.

At the three o'clock in the morning of Monday 15 January they set out from Beas. The weather had cleared but the track was waterlogged.

With Juan and Ana were six nuns, a friar called Pedro, and some mules. For the first few hours the mules could only stagger forward, their hooves sinking deep into mud and clay and slipping on greasy rocks. Somehow they struggled up onto the long ridge that runs south-west towards Baeza. They covered only eight leagues, seven would have been the distance of a marathon, before stopping to rest overnight in Torreperogil. It must have taken them much longer than the standard eight hours walking.

Next morning they carried on three and a half leagues, past Úbeda to Baeza. Here they turned due south for another four and a half leagues, across the Guadelquivir valley to Bedmar, crouching beneath its castillo. They were probably travelling much faster now than on the first day. The Sierra Almadén blocked their way with no track over its 7,000 feet. To the west they would have had to go a long way round via Mancha Real to

Carchel, a distance of nine leagues. To the east they could get just as far south in five and a half leagues, passing not far from Huelma. This is probably the route they took, and it probably meant sleeping out in the hills under the open sky.

The next day they moved on through Guadahortuna and Iznalloz to Deifontes, where they spent the night of 17 January. In the last two days, in foul conditions and the limited daylight of winter, they had covered twenty-one and a half leagues, 120 kilometres. Good mules, and good nuns too.

In Deifontes they worried about how they might be received in Granada. The archbishop of the city was, they knew, not enthusiastic about yet another convent arriving to live off the charity of this crowded provincial capital. They had not received permission from him. They risked not being popular.

Early the next day their arrival in Granada was heralded by an angry storm with almighty thunderclaps. A thunderbolt destroyed the library next to the bedroom in which the archbishop was sleeping. It also killed some of his mules in their stable. It made the archbishop ill with the shock.

So this day of the storm they crept just two leagues forward to Albolete, close by Granada. Here they were surprised to meet their own Vicar-Provincial of the descalzo Carmelites – the man who had ordered them to Granada. He had bad news. The archbishop was showing no sign of coming up with permission for them. And now the landlord of the house they were to occupy had found out what he was letting it to, a convent, and had withdrawn from the contract.

The Vicar-Provincial had found an alternative solution. A noble widow had volunteered her own premises and had already fitted out one of her rooms as a chapel. So Juan must lead his little troop into the city clandestinely and hide them away in the widow's house.

After midnight on 20 January 1582, they set out on their last league to the great, Moorish, fortified Puerta de Elvira, the western gate through the walls into Granada. The only entry into this massive, crenellated, windowless block, was the horseshoe arched gateway itself, closed by mighty, armoured, oaken doors and iron bars. Somehow the way was opened to them – perhaps the Vicar-Provincial had influence – and in they came to clatter down the narrow Calle de Elvira, all its houses darkened, shuttered and bolted up, to reach the welcoming home of their rich benefactress before dawn.

Following Juan, his friar called Pedro, his six nuns and his good mules, I am still a long way behind. I spend the night in Baeza in his old hospital that has metamorphosed into my new hotel.

In the morning, once out of the city, I head downhill for two leagues, two hours under a cloudless sky. I have been told that there will be 'mucha calor'. They say it will reach 35° centigrade. On both sides of the road are well cared-for olive plantations. Some of these old trees squat on twisted trunks whose bases are three feet across. Between the trees the earth is brown, and in some places almost white. For kilometre after kilometre this is a landscape of olives. Only an occasional tractor passes.

There is a crisis in the rural economy here this year. Large tracts of trees have been found to be unpollinated after the cold and wet late spring. They have not flowered and will not bear fruit. At the same time, the market price of olive oil has fallen to a level 30% below what it was two years ago.

I see my first dead snake of the day and then a hare runs across the road. There are swifts flying above until I am well clear of the town, and then swallows, martins, and hoopoe and a green woodpecker, father of Faunus, the Latin version of the great god Pan. There are bursts of colour beside the road, wild flowers, butterflies too.

Across this wide valley I am faced by the Sierra Almadén, over 7,000 feet high and joined at the hip to the Sierra Mágina. No road crosses these ranges so I will go left around the eastern shoulder, which is the way that I think Juan must have gone. I wonder how, in that wild dark winter, he was able to find his path without the maps and the sign-posts that make it easy enough for me.

Two leagues on, I come down to the stone bridge across the Rio Guadalquivir. Was it here for Juan, I wonder? It looks old enough. The central span has been replaced by iron girders. The dark green water flows slowly. Two days walk to the East, upstream, the desecrated spring of El Calvario still loses itself in this turgid current.

Across the river a white Guarda Civil jeep is hiding in the bushes. A man in uniform, with a gun, gets out. This feels like a sinister encounter, resonant with the shootings and dumpings of the civil war. I over-react and, all smiles, I volunteer almost my whole life story.

Now it is uphill for the rest of the day and, even for Spain, it is hot, almost blood heat. Inferno. The road has degraded, a bit broken, gritty and empty. Just before the foothills enfold my track, I can look back and see so clearly Baeza on its ridge, four hours walk behind me.

To be on the road in these conditions is conducive of a state of nada. Nada blocks out awareness of the heat, the glare the uphill slope, the grit under my sandals and burning soles, the sweat in my eyes. After each league, a swig at my big water bottle. I am making for Bedmar.

The ruin of the castillo that stands above the town comes into sight and then, for the next hour, tantalisingly shows itself and hides again as the road winds up to left and right.

In all today's walk, not only do I not go through anywhere but I do not even pass anyone's front door.

Bedmar is hemmed in by steep rock faces. Above the town a great crag stands up to over 4,000 feet. Hidden away, there are caves, caves of the wind, Cuevas del Aire. A future Spanish ambassador to Venice, the marquis of Bedmar, was only ten years old when Juan came through here, and the boy's name was Alfonso de la Cueva.

Bedmar is yet another little olive oil town. The streets are white, steep and narrow. I look for the sign-posted Centro Commercial Garcia Lorca. All I find down this cul-de-sac is a thin white horse in an enclosure that seems to be giving up on being a vegetable garden and becoming, instead, an urban rubbish dump. I ask a boy in a football shirt if there is a hostal in this town. He points and runs ahead. Around the corner there is no sight of him. And this is another dead-end. Finally I am sent in the right direction by an old lady.

In my hostal's restaurant ten middle aged customers are still lunching at a long table, for it is the weekend. The women all sit at one end and the men at the other. At the point where the genders meet sit the youngest woman and the liveliest man.

The family who run this place, in which I take a room are helpful to me, practical and kind, but with never a smile. They don't understand strangers, I think, and they don't like not understanding them. However each time I finish a short conversation with the patrón he pats me gently and reassuringly on the shoulder.

The next morning, on the road early for another hot day, I find that I soon break out of Bedmar's hemmed in hide-away. At first there are pretty foothills and then I turn south to walk along the eastern flank of the mighty Sierra Mágina., The morning air is extraordinarily clear and the views are extraordinarily fine. Great mountains rear up to my right. Below me to my left is a steep, romantic valley where a clear, small river rushes. The landscape is too sharp for olive groves. There are trees of every kind and flowering bushes, rocky crags and tumbling streams. High up on the bare slopes, above the tree-line, are occasional little clusters of white houses. Hoopoes call from somewhere above me, and below, down by the water, I hear turtle doves. Suddenly I am looking down on a bird of many colours flying along the river, as colourful as a kingfisher, yet as big as a hawk, azure and rust, some black perhaps. Far from domesticity, a small, striped wild cat sprints across my path.

I feel so lucky to be out here with all this created world around me. It is like a fulfilling prayer simply to be afoot here. 'In what does prayer consist?' Juan had asked a young sister in the convent at Beas. 'In looking at the beauty of God and rejoicing that he has it,' she had replied. How Juan must have come to love this road which, although he first travelled it in winter's dark, he later saw in all its glory, time and again, in his years of journeying to and from his priory in Granada. He wrote of the divine blessing of such a landscape, in his Spiritual Canticle:

> Scattering grace thousandways,
> He went over these downs at a pace,
> And going by with a gaze,

Just a glance from his face
Clothed them with beauty's trace.

Eventually I come down to earth, down into the foothills where the olive plantations are on the march again. With the mass of bare mountain at my back I turn off Juan's camino onto a messy track of roadworks where dust and grit swirl in the hot wind. It leads me, footsore, into a scruffy little Andalusian industrial centre in the throes of a religious fiesta. I find a cheap restaurant where the most disgusting meal of a lifetime is set before me, albeit at the cheapest price ever. By eight o'clock in the evening the waiters are all staggeringly drunk. In the town's one hostal I experience the most grudging reception of a lifetime. I spend a hot and smelly night in a tiny room for which I am charged the tiny sum of 15 euros, 12 pounds sterling.

Back on Juan's road to Granada, in the morning, I am surprised to find that the olive bearing hills soon give way to a great high swell of rolling wheat fields, daubed with the intense scarlet sheen of poppies. Just as surprising is the whiteness of the year-round snows, straight ahead, on the distant heights of the Sierra Nevada, the massive range that is neighbour to the city of Granada. In a dip the town of Guadahortuna feels as if it has not much changed since Juan came through. I should have stayed here overnight. Perhaps Juan did.

And so the road toils on towards Iznalloz. Gradually the wheat fields give way again to the dark-green monotony of the hills of regimented olive trees.

I clamber up into Iznalloz which strikes me as a little town which should be helping the police with their enquiries. In the steep and narrow cobbled streets men in straw hats stand around all day and stare. On the wall of a house I see a painted swastika. And on another the sign of a blood-red hand. The red right hand of vengeance of which Milton wrote? A big plastic sign beside the door of the town hall announces:

Esto Ayuntamiento
NO TOLERA
la VIOLENCIA
CONTRA las MUJERES
NO la TOLERES TÚ

This town council does not tolerate violence against women, don't tolerate it, YOU.

On the way downhill out of town, with some relief, on the road to Deifontes I visit a 16th century Ermita, a chapel which I am sure Juan must have visited too. It contains an ancient portable figure of Our Lady of the Remedies who might have been able to provide some solace for my aching bones. But the place is locked against me.

From here the dull road towards Granada marches in step with the railway under a great hump of rock on the right. Within three leagues, soon after Deifontes, the tentacles of Greater Granada have reached out to get a grip on it with dual carriageways, flyovers and industrial estates, definitely not clothed with beauty's trace. My final approach to Granada has been so different from Juan's, but has become just as unpromising.

# 16   TO AND FROM THE HOLY MOUNTAIN

I see my first road signs in Arabic.  And there are pomegranates in the gardens, granadas in Granada.  It is a long way in through the suburbs to the old city.

Suddenly I am looking up at the great Moorish block of the Puerta de Elvira.  The Iberians first called the city a name that sounded something like this.  Then the Romans gave it a name that sounded something like that.  The Visigoths copied them.  Then the Muslims Arabised it to Elbira.  But once they had their gardens established they changed the name to pomegranate – Granada.

The horseshoe arch is set high over a broad gateway.   I jink in past some temporary hoardings and I'm in the narrow and interesting Calle de Elvira, with its Arab shop names and its women and girls in headscarves about the place.  10% of the population now are muslim, known as new muslims since the original God-fearing population was driven out in successive purges between 1492 and 1570 – a time when, Brenan says, 'the triumph of the Cross had turned this once prosperous city into a camp and a brothel'.

The Calle de Elvira runs straight and narrow three-quarters of a kilometre to the heart of the walled city.  Somewhere along it was the house where Juan installed Ana de Jesús and her nuns, marked outside by a famous stone watering trough with a bull carved on it, the Pilar del Toro.  But when I do eventually find the stone trough it is no longer in Calle de Elvira but in a nearby square called Santa Ana.  It has been moved.  Tramps and the homeless now drink from it and wash themselves and their clothes there.

The young people in the cafés look crisp, fresh and attractive.  These Andalusians spend a great deal of time sitting around in groups, talking in a desultory way and having cups of coffee now and then, rather as Arabs do.  A girl at a nearby table lets her sandal drop from her foot and straightaway a stray dog has snatched it and run off.  A young man gives chase into the crowds and comes back five minutes later with the shoe.

As usual, the Tourism Office people know nothing about Juan or about any traces there may be of his six-year contribution to the history of Granada as prior, poet and mystic. They suggest I ask at the Carmelite convent, which turns out to be of the shod variety rather than descalzo. It also turns out to be in a war-zone of pneumatic drills and cement mixers. My courage fails me. What am I going to shout into the strange, dumb-waiter revolving cupboard in my bad Castilian, anyway?

Instead, I go to the cathedral that Isabel and Ferdinand commissioned victoriously on the site of Granada's great mosque. It is a church very well disguised as a seat of power, a political building like the Capitol in Washington. I wonder what Juan thought of it. In the cathedral's museo I find a half-size but very life-like model of a friar looking up at me beseechingly. And looking a lot like Juan. But no, the supervisor insists it is San Geronimo. Is there any record here of Juan? No.

I visit the Alhambra in a group, mass tourism in slow motion. Very beautiful. Our guide has a degree in history and tourism but she knows nothing of Juan.

I go on a guided walking tour of the city. Very interesting. I ask this guide about Juan in Granada. He can only shake his head, spread his hands and smile ruefully. He tells me that his own name is Israel.

Wandering north-west from the cathedral I come upon a fine building, a monastery of delicate white stone against the blue sky. This building is popularly known as the house of the Gran Capitán because a great warrior was buried here after helping to throw the Moors out. It is open to visitors. In the centre of it is a garden of orange trees, with a stone-arched cloister all around. Above are smaller arches and a balustrade of delicate, trellised stonework. And above them are further galleries of even finer white stone. This lovely place was where Juan was eventually able to settle his nuns after two years in Calle de Elvira. He took part in the negotiations for the purchase of their quarters himself. And, after that, he was a visitor virtually every week to care for Madre Ana de Jesús and her sisters. In the English language pamphlet handed out here now there is not a single reference to any of them, or indeed to any Carmelite presence at all. 'The community of Nuns of St Jerome who live in the Monastery would like to welcome you and apologise for not being able to attend you personally, due to our contemplative way of life'.

I head back past Calle de Elvira and uphill into ancient, tiny streets, where, seeing a church door open, I go in. The front section of this small church, the east end with altar, is completely caged off by iron bars from floor to ceiling. Beyond the bars there are several nuns, contemplative but visible. They kneel with their backs to me, dressed all in white with their faces veiled. They keep up a constant muttering. Later I find out that, for several centuries, the nuns of this convent have not stopped for a moment  their praying in this quiet little church. They have kept up a continuous relay all day and all night long, all through the years, taking turns. As old ones die, young ones take up the round. And so it will go on for ever and ever, amen – no finish, no end to it, no closure, no term. Another nada-type concept. Endless, like some Spanish landscapes., This is the Congregation of the Slaves of the Most Holy Sacrament of the Immaculate One.

It is time for me to search out Juan up on his holy mountain, his hill-top beside the Alhambra above Granada.

In fact, Juan's hill-top was separated from the Alhambra's hill-top by a deep gorge. Juan's hill was called Los Mártires in honour of all the Christian victims who had died there at the hands of the Moors. It had been a sort of prison camp, a death camp. The Moors had used forced labour to dig out a series of pits in the hillside, wide at the bottom with overhanging inside walls rising to a narrow opening at the top. The prisoners were dropped into these dark, subterranean cones, out of sight and out of mind. Many had died there. So, this place was sanctified by its Christian martyrs and had become the home of the descalzo Carmelite monastery of Los Mártires.

The priory building itself had originally been a small hermitage built by Isabel to honour the Christian martyrs. This had now been slightly enlarged and the barren hill had been to some extent cultivated, and water had been collected in a pond. The digging always turned up bones. Behind the site the mighty Sierra Nevada stood up in snow to over 10,000 feet. In front, the ground fell away sharply to the towers, courtyards and gardens of Granada below, and to the vale of green, fertile farms beyond, the vega. To one side, across the canyon, the golden walls, oriental fountains and pleasure gardens of the ineffable Alhambra. Los Mártires was a fitting seat for a saint and doctor of the universal church. It was here that Juan put the greater part of his prose works on paper, setting out his theology largely in the form of commentary on his poems. And here his soul sang with yet more poetry.

When Juan arrived the friars had been without a prior for some time. There were no more than ten religious and two lay brothers. They fixed happily on Fray Juan de la Cruz and elected him Prior of Granada. Soon novices began to arrive to join the community. They found him to be a wonderfully kind little shepherd to them all.

Humility was the first lesson he taught them by example. A difficult lesson, because the dark side of humility is pride, the great temptation of the ascetic life. Lead us not into temptation. To be able to choose, in humility and without pride, the smallest portion, the dirtiest chore, the narrowest cell. Juan's cell was indeed the narrowest, and it was in the junior quarters among the novices. It was furnished only with a brushwood mattress, a cross, a Bible and a breviary. But it had a small window that looked out onto the vegetable garden and across the great, green spaces of the vega below. He spent much time at this window, day and night, kneeling in prayer. Outside, he tried to pass unnoticed and unconsidered through the world, unobtrusive, silent, his eyes downcast. To confess his sins he would often choose to go to one of the most junior of friars.

Here at Los Mártires Juan's good nature expanded and flowered. He brought a new gentleness to the caring that his friars and the wider community outside his priory experienced from their spiritual director. He was happy and so were they, mostly.

He could not bear to see any unhappiness in his flock and he would take the sad one off for a walk in the countryside to divert and comfort him. He would never forget to ask how each was feeling, how was their physical well-being. His particular tenderness was for the sick, coaxing an invalid into sustenance, perhaps a small rasher of bacon, some cherries and a little wine, while he and the healthy brothers shared a dish of chick-peas and stewed nettles.

He preferred to work through individual, personal relationships, through empathy, than through general discourses. Each night he would go apart with one person for a long, private conversation, so that everyone in the priory knew that their own special time with him would be soon. And, rather than instruct, he advised.

One thing that Juan advised them was not to be hankering after the spiritual favours, the divine insights, that contemplatives might expect God to reward them with. It was enough to endure in quietness, self-sacrifice, patience, humility and even spiritual aridity, to empty their consciousness of everything that was not love, and all insensibly their emptiness would be filled with God's presence.

As for himself, he said that, while a Prior ought not to seek to reprimand all faults he ought not, either, to overlook them all. It was his duty not to hide people's faults from them, but when he corrected them it was with charity, like a father they said. And he always encouraged them to speak up for each other, in explanation or defence. Where possible, he corrected people just with a hint, a movement or a cough, rather than with a reprimand. And where the rules of the Order demanded a penance Juan would soften its interpretation.

They all praised his marvellous way with words. It was poetic. He used to hold them spell-bound and raise their spirits. So they liked him to sit down on the ground among them after the mid-day meal and tell them stories that, in a deft and cheerful way, threw light on the messages of the holy scriptures. This was the way of Jesus with his parables among the disciples gathered around him.

On feast days he would picnic with them all, sitting in a circle on the ground, with perhaps rice and fruit added to their basic menu of bread, herbs, chick-peas and the occasional sardine. And he would talk of man's relationship with God in ways that made them smile. Days when food was short were used by Juan to help his friars in another way. 'Learn to trust in God'.

He loved to take them out to ramble on the hill-sides around Los Mártires and then split up to pray alone. Anywhere you pray, he would tell them you may turn away from the external world and seek God in the darkness of nada: nada of the senses and nada of the spirit. But here you may approach God, too, through todo, everything, the hills, the trees, the

161

flowers and the birds, calling on all the beauty of created things to praise God. 'Oh all ye works of the Lord, bless ye the Lord: praise Him and magnify Him for ever'.

'What is God?' he asked a lay brother whose simplicity and child-like spirit he admired. 'God is what he wants to be,' the man said. Juan loved this reply. This short affirmation could provide him, and any of us, with an opening to explore in repeated and endless meditations. 'God is what he wants to be'.

So, up on his mountainside in Los Mátires, Juan lived a life of loving God and his neighbour as Jesus had asked him to. And his neighbours, loving him in return were helped to love God and each other through him.

Down below, in the city, there were always Ana de Jesús and the nuns to be tended to in the great house of the Gran Capitán. Teresa their founder had recently died, in 1582, after two years of failing health far away in Old Castile. They felt themselves lucky to have kept some small things of hers she had left with them on a visit to Beas. These relics were used by the nuns to help restore Juan to health when, visiting them one day, he fell suddenly and seriously ill during an epidemic of the plague in Granada.

Juan also had two houses of Carmelite beatas to care for. All the women noticed that he made no distinction between them in age, learning or rank. He simply gave more attention to those who were in more need. He was never in a hurry, always listened. Many in the city sought him out for spiritual direction, from masters of the university to poor illiterates, men and women. There were many who venerated him and who called him the holy brother, and some who would try to kiss his hands and feet. Some people even competed to drink the water and eat the crumbs he might have left at table. And, yet again, he was called to draw the devil out of women possessed.

Back up in Los Mártires, Juan somehow found the time and the patrons to put in hand great improvements to the monastery.

Much work was done, so that the buildings were enlarged and the former hermitage developed into a spacious monastery. Juan himself was skilled only enough to work at making sun-dried bricks. His brother Francisco was here to help too. Francisco had come south to join Juan some time after their mother had died in Medina del Campo. The amiable Francisco, now in his fifties and still illiterate, laboured for the master masons. He was a great comfort and support to Juan, who said of him, 'He is the treasure I most value in the world'.

The two major projects were an aqueduct and a cloister. The aqueduct was built to bring a steady and controlled supply of sweet, fresh water from a spring on the hillside and across a ravine into the monastery's large pool and cisterns. Of the cloister, a leading man of Granada wrote that it was the best cloister in Spain in the monasteries of the descalzo Carmelite Reform: 'With its solidity – for it is made of stone – Fray Juan so combined the nobility of the architecture and the beauty of the lights [arches and windows] with decency, devotion and moderation, that when one raises one's eyes it always seems new.' What an aspiration for architecture that is: 'when one raises one's eyes it always seems new'. And what a legacy created on the hill of the martyrs.

Up here on this mountainside, high above Granada a poem of soaring flight came to Juan. It was a poem of the solitary falcon in the hunt. Once again the soul was hunting for its sublime love. Like an eagle reaching the heights, up out of the body flew consciousness, and up out of consciousness flew the spirit, and up out of the spirit the soul, to God. The poem described a trip into mystical exaltation.

> Out for a loving coup
> And not of hope too shy,
> I flew so high, so high,
> In the chase that I reached it too.
>
> To give that strike its due
> As a blessed blow divine,
> I so much took to flying,
> That I lost myself from view;
> And all entranced to go,
> My flight line was undone;
> But so high was the love to be won,
> That I chased and reached it so.

When higher I had risen,
My view was dazzled by rapture,
And so my strongest capture
Was made with darkened vision;
But for this to be love's coup
I leapt in the dark without sight,
And drove so high, such height,
In the chase that I reached it too.

The higher that I went
In this so sudden steep,
The more the strain was deep
And I found myself despondent.
I said: None there shall go;
This struck me so with fright,
That I drove so high, such height,
And chased and reached it so.

In such a manner so strange
All in one passed a thousand flights,
For in hoping for heaven's delights
Hope itself gives reach its range;
I hoped only for that one coup,
And in hope I did not go shy,
Since so high I did go, so high,
In the chase that I reached it too.

In hope I did not go shy, so high I did go, so high, in the chase that I reached it too. This is my aspiration as I start the steep climb to Los Mártires, to reach whatever of Juan is still to be found up there.

The path takes me up hundreds of feet through trees before delivering me on to flat and open ground at the top. To my surprise there is a small car park. Two men talking here turn to greet me in a friendly way. I recognise one of them as the very formal and impressive head waiter of a restaurant down in the centre of Granada, with the battle-hardened face of an emperor. Now he seems to be completely out of character for he is wearing white shorts and a pink shirt and, unusually for a Spaniard, he is very drunk. The other turns out to be an insistent shoe-shine man. He is determined to shine the straps of my sandals, but I am more determined not to let him. He needs the money, he has children to feed – more likely grandchildren by the look of him – so I give him the money and he agrees to leave my sandals alone. We part on the best of terms, although he says he knows nothing of Juan.

The open space on top of the hill of Los Mártires has been turned into a small public park. At first I can find no trace of Juan's priory. I ask a policeman on patrol and I ask a man who seems to be the head gardener but neither of them has heard of it. Then, on a small stone plinth tucked away in a flower-bed at the furthest end of the gardens, I find a bronze head that claims to be Juan. It is rather handsome and reminds me of someone, perhaps a film star, but it doesn't remind me of Juan. It was put here by the Ciudad de Granada in February 2,002.

I encounter another gardener, a young man, and I tell him that I am looking for the remains of Juan's Carmelite priory. He can't help. Then I mention the aqueduct. He can immediately direct me to it, although he doesn't know who put it there. I find it to be in apparently perfect condition, well-maintained as a feature in the park and still carrying water off the mountainside. At its end is a large pool, the priory's pond, but where is the priory and where is the cloister, the best descalzo Carmelite cloister in Spain that 'always seems new'?

I have read that at some stage a terrace of rather fine houses was built along the south-west rim of the flat top of the hill of Los Mártires, that the finest of them became the home of the British Vice-Consul and that its garden contained the picturesque ruins of the priory. But, for all my searching about, no such terrace, garden or ruin is there.

I find the south-west rim of Los Mártires to be occupied now by a great, big, ultra-modern Manuel de Falla (1876-1946) Centre, with exhibition halls, archives and an auditorium. I buy an entry ticket and wander about its stylish empty spaces. I am the only visitor. So, to make room for this white elephant, dedicated to a twentieth century composer of the second rank, or so it seems, to me, the remains of the priory and cloister of St John of the Cross have been bull-dozed into dumper trucks and carted off into oblivion.

At least the magnificent view, Juan's view, across the golden stonework of the city of Granada, far below, and out over the green vega to distant mountains, is still there for me to cherish.

It was up here that Juan composed the final verses of his Spiritual Canticle, the story of a Bride's search, his soul's searching for and finding the Bridegroom, the Beloved, Christ, God.

> BRIDE
> Oh you maidens of Judah!
> Since the roses and flowers in array
> Are scented with amber,
> Out beyond you must stay,
> And not seek to set foot in our doorway.
>
> Oh my Darling, now hide,
> Set the light of your eyes on the mountains
> And in silence abide,
> But watch for the companions
> Of the one who travels strange islands.
>
> BRIDEGROOM
> The white pigeon above
> With the bough to the Ark has returned,
> And now the turtle-dove,
> That mate she so yearned,
> On the green riverside has discerned.
>
> In solitude she bided,
> And in solitude has placed now her nest;
> And in solitude was guided,
> Where alone she loved best,
> He too by love's solitude distressed.
>
> BRIDE
> Loved One, let's delight,
> And let's see your beauty show
> On the heath and bushy height
> Where pure waters flow;
> Deeper within the thicket let us go.

And later, on the fell,
By caverns of rock we shall fare,
That are hidden so well;
And shall enter there,
And with fresh wine of pomegranate us endear.

There to me you will show
For what my soul has striven,
And on me later bestow
There, You, in me living,
What to me on that day has been given.

The breath of air,
The nightingale's sweet descant,
The downs so dear,
The night so silent
In the flame that consumes without torment.

Which none contemplated,
Not even Aminadab's sorties,
And the circling abated,
And the charioteer's horses
Went down to gaze on the watercourses.

The last verse is especially obscure. Aminadab is mentioned in Solomon's Song of Songs, Juan's original inspiration for his own love song, The Spiritual Canticle. The song of songs says, 'I went down into the garden of nuts to see the fruits of the valley, and to see whether the vine flourished and the pomegranates budded [granadas again!]. Or ever I was aware, my soul made me like the chariots of Amminadib [note different spelling]'. Juan suggests a hostile Aminadab, the adversary who has been besieging the soul but whose horses – the passions of the senses – finally come down to be purified by the divine waters, to be baptised as it were.

As I leave the hill of Los Mártires I meet my shoe-shine man again. He comes smiling towards me. He holds my hand between his two hands and laughs out in delight at the solitary walker who pays to have his sandals not cleaned. He is happy to see me on my way.

With Juan, on the other hand, people were happy to see him on his way back. When he had been away the news of his return always ran ahead of him. His people hurried joyfully down the hill to greet him, to kiss his hand and to congratulate each other on seeing him again. He responded with affection. He was one of those singular characters who make people feel happy just at the sight of him approaching. Mandela, perhaps, is another. And there were many homecomings during Juan's six years at Los Mártires, for Juan's duties in the Carmelite Order called him to travel again and again, the length and breadth of Spain.

Juan always travelled light, sometimes alone and sometimes with a friar or lay-brother as companion. Sometimes they simply walked and sometimes they took turns to ride on a donkey or a mule – never taking more than one. As they went, Juan would read the Bible or sing hymns and psalms. Sometimes he would sink into deep prayer and, if it happened to be during his turn to ride, was liable to topple off when the beast stumbled. More often than not he would be travelling in extreme weather, either the inferno of high summer on the Castilian meseta or the invierno ice and blizzards of winter in the Andalusian mountains. Bears and boars roamed free and wolves prowled on the edges of towns. Rivers in spate would have to be forded. Steep and lonely paths in bandit territory would have to be navigated. Once, in the dark, he fell from a cliff but somehow saved himself by clutching at bushes. Another time the friar who was with him fell and broke his leg.

Juan was now in the last decade of a life of famine rations, of cruel conditions and of driving body and soul to the edge. He was physically worn down, frail sometimes to the point of sickness. Once, when passing through the city of darkness, Toledo, he fell ill and had to pause for a few days. I wonder whether he visited the hospital Santa Cruz that had sheltered him so kindly after his escape from Father Tostado. On another occasion he was forced to stop near Córdoba with an abscess in one lung. He chose to disagree with the doctors who told him he was dying. Of his eventual death, which he so much prized, he said, 'The stone for such a holy edifice is not sufficiently well polished'.

At night, where an inn was available Juan would shelter in it, sleep on the ground and eat only if something was offered to him. Otherwise he fasted. Once when he had left an inn a colleague happened to stop there soon afterwards and found himself being asked by the innkeeper and his customers if he knew who the saint was who had just passed that way.

Inns were places of incident, full of heat and smells, noise, singing and fighting, where water was often dearer than wine. They were known as ventas. Around a common table, to which most brought their own food, the travellers developed the art of making a little conversation go a long way, for no-one would choose to brave the terrors of Spain's vast outdoors at night if he could help it.

Outside an inn five leagues north of Granada Juan found two men fighting with knives. He came up to them and cried out, 'By the power of our Lord Jesus Christ, I order you not to fight any more'. With that he threw down between them a hat he happened to have been carrying. The two men stopped fighting. Next he had them embrace and kiss each other's feet in forgiveness. They must have been amazed.

In another inn Juan was called to give confession to the inn-keeper's dying and repentant son who had been stabbed through the chest in a fight.

Outside an inn at Alcolea, beside the Guadalquivir, a prostitute was lewdly soliciting for custom when Juan and his companion arrived. Juan told her that since Christ had redeemed her soul with his blood she should do better. She fell senseless to the ground. When she recovered, she headed off to Córdoba where she married and became a lay-sister with the Franciscan Order, for the rest of her life.

Juan's first journey out of Los Mártires was to a Chapter meeting in Almodóvar (where I had been confused by all the San Juans) in 1583, a trek of some 45 leagues, 250 kilometres, with the dreaded Despeñaperros gorge to be negotiated. At the meeting he argued for all priors like himself to serve one term of two years only and then not be eligible for re-election. He did not want to see a caste of professional and permanent managers emerge. He was over-ruled. And he was criticised for not making enough fund-raising visits to the rich of Granada. He commented that his visits to them were better spent in spiritual work and that his fund-raising time was better spent in his cell, 'asking our Lord to move such persons'. For it seemed to work.

His next trip was to Lisbon for another Chapter meeting. This was three times as far to travel. Here he was elected one of the order's four definitors. These were the chief persons of authority under the Provincial, people who defined things for the organisation. When he left Lisbon he had to go, via Seville, all the way to Málaga – Atlantic to Mediterranean – to comfort the nuns who were in distress over an accident to one of their number, or possibly an attempted suicide. Then it was back to Los Mártires.

He was quickly summoned to a meeting in Pastrana, via his old college in Baeza. Pastrana is west of Madrid, 500 kilometres, 90 leagues, 90 hours walk from Granada. In Pastrana Juan was appointed not just a definitor but the Vicar-Provincial of Andulusia. This would mean frequent pastoral trips around his province. He must visit each monastery and each convent, seven of each, at least once a year.

In August 1586 he was back again from Los Mártires to a meeting of definitors in Madrid. Soon after this he was in Córdoba to found a monastery, and then in La Manchuela for the same purpose. In between, he had been in Seville to open a convent. In November he visited the convent in Málaga. In December, at last, he was back home in Los Mártires for a few days, with well over 1,000 kilometres behind him since he was last there.

Over Christmas and new year, Juan had a flurry of activity with his descalzos in Caravaca in Murcia, in Beas de Segura, so close to El Calvario, and in Bujalance, near Córdoba. Here, in January, he received a message summoning him north to Madrid. It was five o'clock on a cold, wet, winter's evening. His friars urged him to rest and build up his strength, but soon after midnight he took to the road. By the beginning of March he was back in Caravaca, on his way to Baeza to draw up a document for his friars in the sanctuary of Fuensanta, over-decorated now, outside dismal Villanueva del Arzobispo.

Six weeks later he was in Valladolid, north of Salamanca, Old Castile, having survived a terrible storm on the heights of the Sierra de Guadarrama above Segovià. He was 750 kilometres and 130 hours on foot from home. Here, at a meeting called The Great Chapter, the exhausted little figure of Juan was stripped of his posts as definitor and Vicar-

Provincial and simply re-confirmed as prior of Granada. While Juan had been so much on the road in 1583,1584,1585, 1586 and now 1587, his colleagues in The Carmelite Reform had been much engaged in internal politics and power struggles.

In June of the following year, 1588, Juan's sixth year based in Los Mártires, the politicians raised him up again at a Chapter General in Madrid and elected him definitor, a member of the Council and prior of Segovia rather than of Granada. By 1 August he was in Segovia, back in his homeland of Castile at last, his homeland of nada, and never to see Granada's Los Mártires again.

On none of these administrative and political journeys do I follow Juan on foot, thousands of kilometres back and forth. As I have found so little trace of him left in Fontiveros, Arévalo, Medina del Campo, Duruelo, Avila, Toledo, Almodóver, La Peñuela, Beas, Baeza and Granada – places he lived in – what could I expect to find in those places he only visited, Lisbon, Seville, Córdoba, Málaga, Pastrana, Madrid, La Manchuela, Caravaca, Bujalance, Valladolid? This is an excuse. But my main reason, of course, is that my walking, my endurance and my courage are not up to Juan's mark. I would never make it, despite the roads being so much less hazardous and demanding for me now than they were for him then. And so much less interesting too.

The roads of Spain held a special symbolism for the sixteenth century (Byron). They were Spain in an exaggerated form. They were ribbons of commotion stretching across vast, silent, largely deserted landscapes ruled by bands of highwaymen, which were often as big and predatory as army squadrons.

People travelled on foot, in litters, by cart, on donkeys, mules or horses according to their station. The carts, carretas, were long, narrow, four-wheeled ox-carts, which were restricted in use by the absence of adequate tracks in the rugged countryside outside the central meseta. It was mules which provided the principal means of transport. One mule equalled ten men (Lynch). The mule in Spain performed the functions of the camel in the East and had something of its morale, which was congenial to the character of its master: The same self-willed obstinacy, the same resignation under burdens, the same singular capability of endurance of labour, fatigue and privation (Ford).   Interminable caravans crawled along under incredible loads of salt, wood, pottery, grain, melons, hams, wool and works of art.

Everywhere were pícaros, meaning cunning rogues, travelling tricksters and cheats, thieves and fugitives (Bennassar).  Merchants tried not to look too wealthy.   Army sergeants shepherded ragged groups of recruits to embarkation ports.   Priests, tax collectors, and dandies mingled with unemployed peasants on the move.   Vagrants and beggars wandered across the countryside, from monastery to monastery, in search of free soup (Lalaguna).   Convicts in chains shuffled towards the galleys. Itinerant magistrates rode self-importantly.   And always there were the muleteers, the strong, sly, stupid men who were the despots of the highways.  Don Quixote, met with all these types and came to blows with most of them, for the best of reasons.

Don Quixote also fell upon a variety of other travellers and set about most of them too – goat herds, shepherds with transhumant  flocks, hog dealers driving swine to market, picadors herding bulls, a travelling barber, penitents on a vow of pilgrimage to bring an end to the drought, Benedictine monks wearing black travelling masks against the dust, mounted troopers of the Holy Brotherhood, a hidalgo like himself with a squire, a fine lady out hawking, couriers (in 1580 the royal post had been opened to the public), a caged cart carrying two lions, a theatrical troupe, puppeteers with an ape, an author of books on liveries, a canon of Toledo (any relation of Juan's, one wonders) and, strangest of all, six churchmen in white bearing torches by night to accompany a coffin from Baeza to Segovia.  It is quite possible that what Cervantes was describing here was an actual encounter he himself may have had with Juan's own corpse.  Certainly, Carmelites from Segovia made a raid to steal it away from Juan's place of death in Andalusia and smuggle it up to their own priory in Castile.   And at a time when Cervantes himself happened to be on the road.

Apart from his own cortège, Juan, living, will have met all such travellers as these.   Juan spent many more weeks and covered much greater distances than Cervantes's Don Quixote did, on the roads of Spain.  All human life was there.

With his transfer from Granada to Segovia, in the summer of 1588, it was time for Juan to stop travelling. He had left a great spiritual – and architectural – mark on Granada during the six years he had been based there. He faced the same opportunity now in Segovia, but he must have sensed he would have less time. In Segovia he must focus. And here he would seek the darkness of nada again.

# 17  IN SEGOVIA –
##     ALL THE KNOWN WORLD TRANSCENDING

In Segovia Juan would again be drawn into the Carmelite muddle of fingers in every pie, ambitious expansion and politics at every turn.  But he would come through it all one more time.  Through to the darkness of nada where he would be able to approach the true end he sought.  And the descalzos themselves would help by chivvying their own little saint away into that darkness, into nada.

In this same year of 1588, as it happened, Spain itself, also through muddle, ambition and politics, would be chivvying its own great armada away into another darkness, the northern storms, the nada of no return.

I have no thoughts of darkness to come as I walk into Segovia through the bright morning air of summer, so clear across the endless meseta of Juan's golden Castile that it brings to mind the vision of Ortega y Gasset: 'Far away the cathedral of Segovia sails amid yellow wheat fields like a great ship dwarfing the small town at her feet'

This city stands alone, on no main route between any great markets or centres of power.  Close to the shearing stations of the Mesta, the seasonal passage of the flocks, it became the major source of woven merino cloth and grew rich in its own right.  It is simpler than Granada and sunnier than Toledo.

It all looks so fine as I come into the lower end of the town, pack on back, staff in hand.  In front of me, the Roman aqueduct.  Granite blocks without mortar or metal clamps to hold them together carry its arches up to nearly 100 feet and away for nearly a kilometre, intact since Caesar Augustus commissioned them.  The aqueduct provides Segovia with its uniquely distinctive vista, closing off the town and framing the hills beyond.  To my left, over my shoulder, I can look up pedestrianised streets towards the cathedral that glows above, completed a few years before Juan arrived.

I follow him happily up, passing a nice little iron statue of him walking on tip-toes.  For once I am not following the old Don too.  But, curiously, I have caught up again with Antonio Machado, that other poet whose heart was always in Old Castile.  After six uncomfortable years in Andalusian

174

Baeza he came here, back to the high plains, to teach and to write, until the civil war years dragged him off to Madrid and to his death in exile.

In front of the cathedral I cross the Plaza Mayor, which is the highest point in the town and a pleasant living space and a meeting place rather than a spectacular setting. From it the narrow Calle Marqués del Arco takes me on and gently down. This was a street Juan knew well because half-way down it is the Carmelite convent of the descalzas, just as it was when he used to come to care for its nuns. At this corner I turn right into the narrower Calle Descalzos. At the bottom, on the left, an alley, the Paseo San Juan de la Cruz. Segovia is proud of its saint and has kept the bulldozers on the leash. What a blessing for me!

This is the path Juan took so often down from the town to his monastery. It is steep and sometimes there are stone steps. It comes out through a doorway in the city walls, Puerta de Santiago. Below is the river Eresma. Across a stone bridge, I follow the bend of the river to the left around a stony spur of land with some buildings beneath. Suddenly, on my right, a tidy garden of gravel, grass and slender evergreens, the approach to Juan's handsome priory. And behind the closed door he is still there in spirit and, partly, in body.

Juan built this place because when he arrived he found that the previous building had been built too close to the river and was cracked and damp. And it was too small for all the projects the Carmelites wanted him to manage in it. He was to increase the numbers of friars significantly from the current seven plus a novice. And he was to add a college of at least twelve students. And he was to accommodate the Council of the Spanish Carmelites and their Vicar-General. So his first and most urgent task was to organise demolition and re-building on firmer footings. For this he needed funds. God provided, in the form of the lady benefactor of the Granada convent, Ana de Peñalosa. She soon followed her money and came to Segovia to live in a small house beside Juan's monastery.

Work began at once. Masons set out the new foundations, day-labourers came down from the city and the friars lent a hand. Behind the site was a garden and an orchard running up to low cliffs. Rock was quarried from these cliffs. Juan supervised, barefoot and bare-headed right through that first Castilian winter in Segovia, through snow and hail. When a friar

175

exclaimed at how at ease he seemed among all this he replied that when dealing with stones he had less to stumble over than when dealing with men. But for those workers who did injure themselves in the heavy labour his patient, hands-on care seemed to give miraculous comfort and healing.

When summer came again the roof was on. Finishing and improving would take months, and even years, but the priory was in business. Juan, of course, took the smallest cell.

Now the shepherd must turn to his flock. The numbers started to build up, more friars, more novices, more lay-brothers, more students. He guided, instructed and corrected them, they felt, in a spirit of fatherly love. They liked him to go among them at recreation and join in their conversations. If anyone spoke ill of others he would leap to their defence. When warned that somebody might not be being entirely honest with him, he commented, 'It is better to let oneself be taken in.' The establishment was a happy one and Juan encouraged it to be so. He helped them make the most of their celebrations, at liturgical feasts and particularly at Christmas.

And then there were the nuns. Once a week he went to hear their confessions, over the bridge, up the steep path, through the narrow gate in the walls, up the Paseo, right into the Calle Descalzos and up to the convent on the corner. Often they found a reason to get him up there between-times because they loved him. They said that when he was with them 'the house became a heaven'.

His presence was felt beyond the walls of the priory and the convent. The great and good of Segovia would clamber down from the city to spend time with him. And he would go out visiting too, responding to invitations. Always he would ensure that the gathering included all members of the household, including the servants. He would listen, he would talk and sometimes he would read to them.

His confessional, squashed in under the stairs of the priory church was a magnet to the people. A regular visitor, a citizen of Segovia, one day saw a great radiance shining out from that cubbyhole. And on two more occasions he saw it. Finally he asked Juan about it. 'Keep quiet, you silly, and don't say anything', was the reply. Another who came was a distinguished and beautiful young woman who wore fine clothes and dyed her hair blond. She saw the radiance too and was then so much impressed by the example of Juan's humble loving-kindness that she responded to it by going home, putting on a coarse serge gown, thick woollen stockings and heavy shoes, cutting off her blond hair and taking to prayers and penance. To the regret of some of her admirers, no doubt.

Intruding into all this love for his neighbour and for God, came the Carmelite business with heavy demands on Juan. The Consulta or governing council of the Order had moved in right under his roof. When the Vicar-General was away, which was often, Juan had to stand in as president of that committee and administer its tentacular practices: nominating descalzos to positions in Carmelite establishments all over Spain, clarifying rules, duties and responsibilities, answering questions, adjudicating in disputes, recording discussions, and agreements, issuing bulletins and so on and so forth. Tiresome, bureaucratic work for a mystic poet. In all of this he was called upon to try and make a virtue of necessity, as Teresa had once put it.

But he was able both to carry it all out and to rise above it. Literally. Half-way up the rock face that rose at the end of the garden and the orchard was a small natural cave, a cleft quite low and narrow. The tiny, open space in front of it was hemmed in with heather, broom and brambles. It was a place of absolute peace and quiet, and of birdsong, humming of bees and the rustling breeze. The view by day was lovely. Below lay the huerta, the gardens, and the monastery itself. Opposite, the river Eresma met a smaller river, the Clamores, beneath a great jutting prow of rock on which stood the fairy-tale fortress of the Alcázar. To the left stood the city on a hill, with its towers, arches and outer walls. In the distance, the mountains of the Sierra de Guadarrama. By night, nothing but the firmament of radiant stars.

Thank God for this place. Only here could Juan be alone, set aside from the urgent world. He believed that in solitude was to be found the truth of the human condition; that all human beings are solitary, however hard they may work at forgetting it (Dombrowski). So our solitude is a state that is shared by everyone. We are united in common solitude and sympathy. Our journey through life, and most of mine through Spain as it happens, is el camino de la soledad. But at our deepest centre of solitude we can find sanctity. Alone in the depth of nada Juan found God there. At the hidden centre of our solitude we can drink from a source, a source of well-being. Brenan, in 'The Face of Spain', recalls going into a church and hearing 'the sermon which was on the importance of preserving an interior solitude (what a Spanish subject!)' What was key was to be able to preserve the truth of that interior solitude even in an active life. One can accomplish true solitude, as Juan did, not by leaving society but by transcending it.

So Juan went up to his little cave, like Elijah on Mount Carmel, and prayed. 'In what does prayer consist?' he had once asked a sister at Beas. 'In looking at the beauty of God and rejoicing that he has it', she had answered. The little cave was just the place for this. For a matter as intimate as opening ourselves to God, Juan said, we should go into our secret places, into gardens, and groves rather than into churches which are furnished for ceremonial. That is why our Saviour chose solitary places for prayer – places that lift up the soul to God, Juan wrote in 'Ascent of Mount Carmel'.

And how did Juan pray? To pray, he said, we need to be free, to become passive, detached, silent, like the atmosphere which the sun warms and illuminates in proportion to its calmness and clarity. Prayer is this state of loving attention (Obbard, 'The Living Flame of Love'). Man's passivity is, in fact, the highest activity, that of creation and discovery (Cugno, 'St John of the Cross'). Christ told his disciples that when they prayed they ought not to desire to speak much since God knew well what they needed. So we should not approach God with multiple petitions but simply persevere in the Lord's prayer in which are included all our needs. But first and principally, in quiet interior solitude, we should wait and keep our watch for God, and then all these other things will be added to us. And even when praying like this does not please us, it may well be pleasing to God. This was how Juan prayed.

Because Juan's life was busier now than ever before, with more and more responsibilities, his inner solitude rose to the occasion and kept him balanced by strengthening its hold on him. When called down from his cave by a friar for an urgent meeting, Juan would sometimes reply, 'Leave me, for the love of God, for I am not in a fit state to transact business with people'. When he did come down he would sometimes be so absorbed in divine things that he could hardly attend to what was being said. He would force himself to concentrate on the matter of the moment, and not drift off it, by knocking the knuckles of his hand repeatedly against the stone wall. He did it so often and so hard that his joints were damaged. At night, in prayer, he would become so withdrawn from the world that no-one could recall him to it by speaking to him, or even by tugging at his habit.

Juan seemed in Segovia to reach a new peak of spiritual ascension, finding God there so directly that all his years of accrued academic lore fell away from him like superfluous gowns and trappings from a true master of science, arts and theology. He tried to record this personal experience in a poem dismissing learning as a means of reaching God. It is not one of his finest. The ecstasy has been blunted in forcing its way out from his interior solitude to become words on paper. My translation, as usual, tries to keep his rhyme scheme, his number of stresses per line, and his thoughts in the lines in which he put them. His word ciencia, meaning the sum of man's knowledge gained by rational, scientific examination of the world about him, I have translated as 'all the known world'.

> When I went in, I knew not,
> And stayed there not comprehending,
> All the known world transcending.
>
> I knew not where I went,
> But when I saw I was there,
> Where I was, without intent,
> Great things were clear;
> To perceive but not to share,
> And to stay not comprehending,
> All the known world transcending.
>
> Of peace and of piety
> The proof was perfect,
> So profoundly solitary
> The conceived way correct;
> The thing was so secret,
> Words will fail me without ending,
> All the known world transcending.

There was I, so involved,
So absorbed, set apart,
Out of mind, dissolved,
Unselfconscious at heart;
And the spirit alert
To a comprehension uncomprehending,
All the known world transcending.

He who gets right to this conviction,
At the same point may faint away;
The higher the known perfection,
The lower it can him lay;
And his knowledge may grow in a way,
That he stays not comprehending,
All the known world transcending.

The higher I progress,
The less is my insight,
And this is the darkness
That gives brilliance to the night;
For with this wisdom it is right
To stay always uncomprehending,
All the known world transcending.

To know it without it making sense,
Has a force so high,
That wise men's arguments
Can never deny;
Learning does not apply
To incomprehension of comprehending,
All the known world transcending.

So high is its excellence,
So supremely comprised,
That there's no skill or science
Which could be so enterprised;
To conquer self and be seized
With a non-comprehension of comprehending,
Is to be always transcending.

And if you wish to hear
What are the supreme elements,
In a flash to be clear
About the divine essence;
It is the workings of his benevolence
To have us stay not comprehending,
All the known world transcending.

Standing where Juan stood, on the steps outside the door of the monastery that he built, I turn and look up at the fine city of Segovia as he looked up at it sometimes.

The door is closed but I can open it. Where I went in I knew not. I find myself in a small hall-way. In front of me more doors stand open into the monastery church. To my right an open door into what seems to be an office with a stern man sitting at a desk. There is also a rack of tasteless religious knick-knacks for sale. I ask the stern man whether photography is prohibido. He replies that it is not and seems to soften up momentarily, perhaps at my being so unpresumptious as to ask. I go into the church.

The interior of the church is dominated by a great, elaborate, gilded stone sepulchre standing on four columns over the altar at the east end. Not Juan's style. It was built nearly 100 years after Juan's death to house his remains. The hugely heavy and ornate stone casket does not look easy to break into. Indeed, parts of him are still safely in there.

Next I look down through a large trapdoor in the polished floorboards of a side-chapel into a brick-lined chamber beneath. A plaque above it, in the wall, says, 'Here was deposited the incorrupt corpse of S. Juan de la Cruz until his beatification in 1675'.

Of most interest to me is a red-painted wooden box, about the size of a large tuck-box from a 1950s prep-school. This is the box that travelled back from Juan's first burial place in Úbeda. This is the box that Cervantes may have met on the road by night, and described Don Quixote meeting. This is the box in which six churchman in white, bearing torches, carried those parts of the body of Juan they claimed for Segovia, after they had dug him up from his first grave and dismembered him: his head, his

181

torso and one arm. The arm was later granted to Medina del Campo, but was mislaid when that city went into eclipse for a couple of centuries.

Here with me in this room, this small monastic church of his, are Juan's perhaps uncorrupted flesh, the bones of his body, his head, his brain, his DNA, in a deep trance, all the known world transcending. I wish I could see what's left of him here. I leave reluctantly.

I go out of the front door of the church and stand beside it, peering up the garden and the orchard towards the cliff at the end. I cannot make out the cave. This garden is prohibido to me.

An only slightly scruffy man is hanging around outside with me. I ask him if one can visit the cave. He says that I will have to ask the man in the office. That stern man emerges a moment later and gives the scruffy man a plastic bag. The stern man seems to be avoiding my eyes although I am standing right beside the scruffy man. The plastic bag looks as though it contains food, and as the only slightly scruffy man turns away I notice that his back is covered in grass. A moment later a much scruffier man emerges from some bushes and looks expectantly at the stern man. I realise that what the stern man is doing is doling out food to tramps. In answer to my question he says that it is not possible to visit Juan's little cave. I later read that it has been transformed into a niche for an altar and incorporated into a small chapel. It is therefore unrecognisable as Juan's cave.

Never mind, I realise that Juan would not approve of my pathetic search for fetishes, to see, touch, sit on, tread on anything he has seen, touched, sat on or trod on. 'The truly devout person sets his devotion principally on what is invisible,' he said.

I wind back up the narrow track into the city. I like the feel of it here just as I liked the feel of Medina del Campo. And, whatever Juan might say about it, it so happens that both places have bits of Juan himself hidden away within them.

But, after Juan's first three years in Segovia, the world of Carmelite politics was coming to pay him a visit again. The Order had developed an issue with Juan, and this was a case of 'cherchez la femme' or 'les femmes' indeed. Ana de Jesús, Juan's old friend, had become spokeswoman for all the descalzas. On their behalf, she had applied for and received from Rome a dispensation that the descalzo superiors should not be allowed to interfere in the nuns' Constitution. The women also proposed that Juan should be appointed their Visitor-General in sole care of their government.

The Vicar-General of the descalzo order responded angrily to having been by-passed in this way and declared that the nuns should simply be left to their own devices, without any Visitor-General, let alone Juan. They should be entirely separated from The Carmelite Order and turned adrift. Juan spoke up against this move in a meeting of the Consulta. He also openly defended another father who had fallen foul of the Vicar-General.

On the first day of June, the eve of Pentecost, 1591 the Chapter of the descalzo Carmelite friars met in Madrid, with Juan present in his role as councillor, a member of the Consulta. The first thing the Chapter did was to elect Juan off the Consulta. So now he would not qualify to be Visitor-General to the Carmelite nuns if ever such a post came into being after all. But he was still prior of Segovia. Talkative new and younger members of the Consulta lost no opportunity in front of the Vicar-General to humiliate this irritating example of quiet saintliness in the noisome political stew.

The next act of the Consulta was to remove Juan from the office of prior of Segovia. He was now just a friar to be got out of the way. It happened that the Carmelites of Mexico had just applied to the Chapter to send 12 religious to help develop that province. This was not a popular posting. Juan was the only person who said he was willing to take on the task. So they appointed him to it with great pleasure. He could end his days out of sight and out of mind in a desert on the other side of the Atlantic Ocean.

Kamen, in 'The Disinherited', writes of the belief that an innate characteristic of the Hispanic mind is the continuous urge to perform a form of surgical purification on its own body. And that they trace this back to the first and most elemental of all crimes, as narrated in the Bible story of Cain who killed his brother Abel out of envy. As Menéndez Pidal, the medievalist, wrote in 'Spaniards in their History', 'In Spain, difference of opinion degenerates into a contest of irreconcilable animosity'. In Castilian they refer to such hostility as Cainismo. Or they refer to the theory of the Two Spains: there are two, and there are always two, two Spains locked in an unending struggle. Some have suggested that this is Spain's particular and original sin. Antonio Machado wrote of it.

| Españolito que vienes | Little Spaniard coming |
| al mundo, te guarde Dios | into the world, God save you. |
| Una de las dos Españas | One of the two Spains |
| ha de helarte el corazón | has to freeze your heart. |

The Vicar-General's Cainismo then wavered. He wanted to send Juan back to run the Segovian priory again. Juan refused: 'God has done me a great mercy in that I shall now take care of my own soul alone.' So the Vicar-General simply assigned Juan to the province of Andalusia, which he had earlier been so pleased to leave. He was to be a simple friar, turned loose to wander alone, not nominated to any particular monastery. In Andalusia he would at least be nearer to ports of embarkation to Mexico, when the time came. And perhaps he might encounter other waifs and strays to make up with him the dozen called for.

When Ana de Jesús wrote to him in sympathy he answered 'That things have not turned out as you wished, you ought rather to console yourself and give much thanks to God, for since his Majesty has ordained it thus, it is what is best for everyone'. And to the prioress of the convent in Segovia he wrote, 'Do not think anything else except that God ordains all things. And, where there is no love, put love and you will draw out love'.

Juan prepared to take to the road yet again, to head south, to leave his homeland of Castile for the last time and wander about in Andalusia, a land always strange to him. He had to say his farewells to his brother Francisco, a man so simple and kindly that his Jesuit confessor in Medina del Campo said of him, 'Francisco de Yepes is as great a saint as his brother.' Francisco had joined him for their last few days together. Juan led his brother, 'the treasure I most value in the world', out into the priory garden to smell the night-time fragrance of the flowers, look up at the panoply of stars and hear the sound of distant waters. He told Francisco that, while contemplating a painting in the monastery church of Christ carrying the cross, he had asked, 'Lord, what I should like you to give me is trials to suffer for you, and to be despised and esteemed of little worth'. He now felt that his prayer was being answered, which was such an honour that it pained him that he did not deserve it.

184

One of the last people Juan said goodbye to was the barber who came down from the city regularly, to shave all the friars. Juan and the barber had a strangely benevolent relationship. The barber, after shaving the friars, would try to leave too quickly to be paid, for he knew they were poor. Juan would ambush the barber with, for example, the gift of a tunic. Or he would trick him into sitting down with the friars to eat. The barber loved to talk with Juan. He felt that, whatever he might say, Juan gave his whole attention to it, with great kindness. He would always leave feeling happy. But this last time made him feel sad. 'When will you be back here?' the barber asked. Juan told him definitely that he would not return. They would not see each other again, unless in heaven.

# 18  LA PEÑUELA – SINCE IT IS A MATTER OF OBEDIENCE, LET US GO

The road to heaven was a long one.  Walking by himself, Juan covered 500 kilometres before taking a rest.

First of all it was a full twelve leagues, twelve hours at a brisk pace, nearly 70 kilometres, to Avila, where I had walked the walls and seen Teresa's finger in a glass case, still wearing a ring that was set with a large, green stone.

Ten leagues on towards the south, 56 kilometres, to Cebreros up in its hills, where Juan had been encouraged in vain by his innkeeper to escape his captors, and where my innkeeper had instructed me to jump out of my window into a flowerbed when I wanted to leave in the morning.

Another nine leagues to Escalona, about as far away from the edge, from any of the edges, as one can get to in Spain, and where I had resisted the temptation to pick up the pistol off the hall table as I let myself out of my scruffy lodging.

Twelve leagues further on crouched 'the clear and illustrious nightmare' of Toledo.

Then there were 21 leagues across the burnt empty spaces of La Mancha before Ciudad Real.  At least two very long days for Juan on a donkey, followed by me on a bus full of sleepy students, the first time we both came this way.

Just eight leagues to the mining town of Puertollano where I, on my bench, had been set upon by flies, moths and heavy rain drops and had then unloaded a raunchy, lesbian, paperback novel onto a very courteous young, black Englishman.  Perhaps Juan made a diversion here to the descalzo priory in Almodóvar.  I had found it to be for sale.

A long 12 leagues further on was Viso whose fine fifteenth century church had sheltered Queen Isabella's coffin for one night and still houses a stuffed crocodile, which was already hanging on the wall when Juan and I first came through.

Finally, just seven leagues to La Peñuela, into Andalusia through the frightening gorge of the Desfiladero de Despeñaperros, the defile of the throwing down of the dogs.

Juan was probably about two hard weeks on the road between Segovia and La Peñuela. It was a distance that, even with my odd lift or bus, demanded at least three weeks out of me, softened by a lifetime of travel on wheels and wings.

While Juan was quietly walking south, a talkative and over-promoted young member of the Consulta back in Segovia, already a definitor at thirty-one, was setting on foot an enquiry against him, a defamatory process designed to throw him out of the Carmelite Order, to deprive him of the habit he had worn so long and so kindly. The young man pressed the nuns of Segovia and the nuns of Granada to provide him with accounts of the sinfulness of Juan's words and deeds. He pressed them with promises, and more often with threats, to speak ill of Juan. When the harassed nuns came up only with declarations of Juan's goodness he edited and falsified their record. He would be too slow with the compilation of his report on Juan to catch him alive with it. And three years later a new Vicar-General would have the malicious fiction burnt in his presence.

But now Juan was cast out into the wilderness at La Peñuela. It was further from the works of man than any other descalzo Carmelite monastery. It was in wild highland country. It was perfect for the solitude and the interior life that he needed. Originally there had been just a small hermitage here inhabited by a handful of solitary monks, united only by their penitential way of life, long beards and black habits. For the last 14 years the descalzos had occupied the place and worked hard at creating a paradise in the wilderness. They had planted seven thousand vines and three thousand olive trees. They had cultivated 150 acres of barley, wheat and oats. They had laid out a huerta, a garden around a spring, with an orchard beside, and in it they had built a new church.

A few days after his arrival he wrote to the benefactress who had funded his building works in both Granada and Segovia that he felt very well and that la anchura del desierto, the vastness of the wilderness, greatly helped both body and soul.

Juan could be as happy here as he had been at once lovely El Calvario. The friars of La Peñuela saw that he was happy and that he was close to God. Every morning he was up before daybreak and out into the huerta to pray. Sometimes he asked leave of the prior to go into the mountains. In lonely places, particularly by springs, he would kneel in divine contemplation until he heard the sound of the bell calling him back into the community, into church. He behaved in all things like the humblest novice of the establishment. Sometimes he would ask permission to go into his cell and write, and there he worked and re-worked the short poem of his death and union with God. 'Complete now will you yet, break through the veil to sweet encounter'.

But could he stay here? He didn't belong here, he belonged nowhere now. He wrote to the Vicar-Provincial of Andalusia, 'Your reverence will decide what you want me to do and where you want me to go'. And again he wrote, 'Your reverence will decide where you want me to go and there I will go'. Go where you like was all the answer he could get. In the absence of any other distraction, and to the joy of the friars around him, he simply stayed at La Peñuela.

From time to time he walked down to Linares, 20 kilometres to the south, to give spiritual comfort to the poor people of that grubby mining town. It is famous now only for the death of the great Manolete in its bull-ring. Linares feels to me like Mexico, but a Mexico whose sky is the colour and the weight of the lead from the mines that gave its men a living while it poisoned them to death.

I must find La Peñuela. I am not on a wild mountainside. I am in 'a jewel of rational urbanisation'. No more wilderness here. I am back in La Carolina. This town has swallowed La Peñuela. It has swallowed Juan too, leaving only his name on the side of its plate, or rather on a small sign saying that he is 'patron de la ciudad' of La Carolina. Not a single book or piece of printed material about him is available in tourist office, church or book-shop. Nobody can tell me anything about him. Finally, the receptionist in a hotel much grander than anything I am accustomed to staying in gives me a very grainy photocopy of the grid system of the town's streets. A sports centre at the top edge of this map is marked by the figure of a man kicking a ball and beside him I can just make out the faint words, 'San Juan de la Cruz'. So I go looking for this footballer, heading north-west and gently uphill from one side of town to the other.

Beyond the centre, in a small square, I come upon a white stone statue of a man in a habit and cloak, holding a small cross to his chest, half crouching and looking down into the flower-beds around him. On the plinth is a date, 24.11.1961, and a name, San Juan de la Cruz. Above the square stands the fine church of the Immaculate Conception. Is this the church that the descalzo Carmelites built for their monastery? The style looks of the right period. No information on this is forthcoming, inside or out. Nor, later, at the tourist office, which is not really a tourist office but a large cardboard box full of tourism leaflets in the Ayuntamiento, the town hall. When I look this word up in a dictionary, I am intrigued to find that, while ayuntamiento means town council, ayuntamiento carnal means sexual intercourse.

At the Immaculate Conception I search about for more signs of Juan. Past the church a narrow street continues to rise and then crests and gently descends. On my right are some empty concrete sports pitches and then a big sports hall. Behind the sports hall is a paved open space with ornamental trees and bushes and some benches. Beyond, the ground falls away into a valley full of small modern housing estates. It is orderly here and peaceful. It feels good. Unaccompanied children come through, on their way home from school for lunch, I suppose, behaving well.

Standing to one side of my quiet, paved, open space, with ornamental trees and bushes and some benches, is a small, white-washed building, clearly religious, with a bell above and a cross on top. It looks ancient but well cared for, with solid stone walls and few very small openings, high up, to let light in. It must be dark inside. It is a hermitage. It is the hermitage that Juan came to in La Peñuela when he was cast out by the descalzo Carmelite Consulta. It even has his name on a little plaque on the wall. The huerta around, the garden, the orchard, the fields may be paved and built over but the site still has a quiet atmosphere. The hermitage is locked but it has not been bull-dozed away. Good for the good people of La Carolina!

I look across the valley to the unchanging contours of the wild mountains above in the high, bright, summer air. I feel exhilarated, standing and looking where Juan stood and looked. I think that I can sense in me some tiny part of his feelings, helped as he was in body and soul by the vastness of the wilderness, la anchura del desierto. But I am so far behind.

Turning back into the mundane, urban centre of La Carolina, I have to come to terms with my own lack of spirituality. What would Juan's soul, so open, so high, so deep, so far, make of my pedestrian progress through life, distracted hither and thither by the devices and desires of my own heart. Well, I have come to trust, through reading him, through writing his poems into English, through rambling over Spain after him, that he was tolerant of the likes of me.

Juan said, in 'Ascent of Mount Carmel,' that what he called 'natural desires' (spontaneous, unintentional, wandering snatches of interest) were innocent distractions rather than serious barriers between man and God. 'They produce no evils in the soul'. He saw how difficult it was 'for those who set out on the road of virtue and make no progress ... remaining in an elementary state of communion with God for lack of will or knowledge.' He, so focussed, understood us in our 'elementary state', the scatter-brained majority. He recognised that there are few who are able to enter, and also desire to enter, into a complete detachment from the world and an emptiness of spirit. He advised that if one cannot meditate one should just practise being still and fixing loving attention on God, here and now, trusting that he understands one. One may think that one is doing nothing, but do it nevertheless.

At the other end of the scale, Juan suggested that there are people into whom God enters with supernatural gifts and graces and to whom he gives the light to see this. Such a soul, he wrote in 'Ascent of Mount Carmel', may be moved to perform acts of mercy in the manner in which God so moves it.

God so moves that soul because he cannot do otherwise. It is simply God being what he wants to be. And thus there may be people through whom small miracles are worked, although it is not God's purpose to perform miracles. Then it may be, perhaps, that a tiny fragment of the hidden higher reality beyond and all around us, a divine spark, pieces the veil from the other side and, on this side, a soul spontaneously lights up the created world through which it moves.

Maybe animals are more sensitive to this spark than men are. One day a hare became trapped in the descalzos' church at La Peñuela. When the doors opened it ran out in fear and, before all the brothers, it leapt up and took refuge in the folds of Juan's habit. A friar took it by the ears and carried it away to release it, but it escaped him and ran for refuge again into Juan's arms. And then there had been the dove, back in Segovia. The friars had noticed that this beautiful bird spent much time perched on a beam above the door to Juan's cell, never flying off with the flock. One of them asserted that he had seen this same dove sheltering in Juan's cell in Granada. Another creature so influenced had been the big fierce dog on the path between Beas and El Calvario. It had run at Juan and his companion as if to attack. 'Don't be afraid', Juan had said to the flinching friar and had simply stretched out his hand and placed it on the animal's head. And the dog was at peace. Shades of Daniel, of Androcles and of Jerome, with their lions. And shades of St Francis of Assisi to whom all God's creatures were his brothers and sisters, and who preached to the birds. Had the monstrous fish which leapt from the water to greet the nine-year-old Juan to Medina del Campo felt something special about him?

The friars at La Peñuela certainly believed that Juan had the gift of performing acts of mercy on their behalf when forces of nature, of the created world, threatened them by chance. After taking their harvest in they had set fire to the stubble. The wind changed and drove the flames towards the monastery. Juan advised the friars to go into the church and pray. He himself knelt in the path of the fire. When the flames reached the place where he was they turned away and died down. The friars came out of the church and found Juan soaked through with sweat and blackened with soot but with a face so happy that 'it stole your heart away', said one. Soon afterwards a great storm approached, so violent that it might destroy the vineyard and the olive grove. Juan told the friars not to worry. Going into the cloister he bared his head and, looking to heaven, traced four crosses in the air, to the four points of the compass. The storm vanished. The descalzos thanked God.

News came to La Peñuela of the campaign of defamation being drawn up against Juan . He would not let the friars talk to him about it. Their resentment of it, he said, gave him more pain than the defamation itself did. He wrote, 'I am more than prepared to make amends for anything in

191

which I may have erred and to accept whatever penance they may give me. Don't let it grieve you'.

Juan had been less than two months, August and September 1591, in lovely La Peñuela when he fell ill with a slight fever. It seemed to arise from an inflammation around the ankle of his right leg. He was 49 years old and he could not shake it off.

He did not want to leave the vastness of this wilderness. But here there were no doctors or medicines. The friars urged Juan to go for treatment in the university town of Baeza. He would not. Twelve years earlier he had founded a college there, taught the students, tended the sick in hospital and cast demons out of the afflicted. He had been a reluctant celebrity there and now he wished to live, and to die when it came to that, in humility and obscurity. Near Baeza was Úbeda with a descalzo Carmelite monastery and 'in Úbeda nobody knows me'. The Superior at La Peñuela ordered Juan to Úbeda. 'Since it is a matter of obedience, let us go,' he replied.

## 19 ÚBEDA – BREAK THROUGH THE VEIL TO SWEET ENCOUNTER

And so I come on down from La Peñuela, breaking out quickly from the tidy streets of La Carolina onto slopes of olive groves. The empty road is familiar until I turn off to the right at little Los Arquillos, on its flat ledge four leagues out. It is a hot high noon. For another two and a half leagues the road winds quietly downhill past olive trees and small dry fields. There are rabbits.

At the Rio Guadalimar I find that the river has been dammed to form a reservoir. The narrow watercourse has become a wide lake. Juan's crossing, an old five-arched stone bridge, is drowned. The new road takes me round the reservoir in a great sweep to a fine, high, steel bridge, at least 100 metres long. Halfway across this stainless structure I find droppings. Rabbit or goat? Why did the animal cross the bridge?

On the far side, the slope of the road looks more demanding. It is a big landscape, not an intimate one, through which I am to follow Juan. For three dusty leagues uphill, a climb of 2,500 feet, I am going to manage less than one league each hour.

The traffic comes down this road on me at great speed, and I can see it coming from a long way off. All this long afternoon, up this long road, the only fellow creature afoot is a thin dog in a ditch eating road-kill remains – something of fur and bones. The dog looks at me with eyes that seem to wish me gone, as a fortunate diner might look at an unwelcome, hungry bystander.

There are olive plantations, of course, and wide open stretches with sheep and goats grazing in the distance. Also some pale, dry ploughed strips. Wild oats by the roadside have turned white in the summer drought.

At last the open road runs straight into a suburb. Its buildings become progressively more antique as I get closer to the Muslim walls of Úbeda. I follow Juan through the walls into the old city. Our gate is the Arab gate of El Losal.

Úbeda is a town of fine old stone, a bright and golden tombstone of a town. Its intricate medieval street plan is punctuated here and there by the restrained assuredness of Renaissance private palaces.  It is quite small.  I walk through handsome parts and, from time to time, I walk through smells of drainage.

The broad square in the centre of the old, walled town is closed in along its northern side by the great church of San Pablo, once a mosque.  Out in the middle is a slender statue of Juan, much too tall again.  Perhaps the authorities feel that it would be disrespectful to portray a great man life-size, at 4 feet 10 inches.

My approach to Juan's death in Úbeda's descalzo Carmelite monastery becomes meandering and diffident, a matter of days not hours.

A young woman looks out of the porch of a small stone palace and sees me hanging about in a studious way in the narrow, cobbled street.  She invites me inside where, for a fee of three euros, she can show me some curious antiquities.  Some are, indeed, very curious and some are ancient.  There are samurai swords and Victorian writing desks, harem beds and saddle stools, 'for ladies'.  There are Moorish wall paintings from the tenth century apparently, and a sixth century Visigothic font.  Edging through yet another roomful of clutter I am shaken by a sudden terrible roaring sound which I take to be some massive engine for building works starting up close by.  But the woman leads me to a curtained alcove and reveals a little braying ass.  We stroke its muzzle.  Chato.  Its name is Mustafa.  Smiles all round.

Outside the big San Pablo church next day I watch a party emerge from a baptism, the baby wearing a long white christening robe.

At the nearby Puerta de Santa Lucia, in the evening, I see a great company of brown and black goats being herded through the walls into the old city.  Where are they going?  I should follow them, but I don't.  I don't want to leave this cluster of little streets around the Carmelite monastery.

At San Pablo a wedding day is celebrated, the bride in white.  A girl throws a handful of rice over me.  I brush it out of my hair and people are amused for I am an odd figure, a burnt-out wayfarer wandering around the edges of a smart, social occasion.  Later there is a funeral in the church.

And on television a death is being celebrated.  Spain's great lady of song, 'no mas grande' they say, has died at only 61.  She has been twice married.

Her first husband was a boxer and her second a torero, Jose Ortego Cano. But in one of her last interviews she spoke of 'the immense solitude of chemotherapy'. Now Spanish television is devoted to public lamentation. Mostly this consists of weeping celebrities in dark glasses embracing each other. The walk to the graveside is impressive. There seem to be 12 men carrying the coffin through the great crowd. It is almost in slow motion. The coffin is piled high with floral tributes. Petals rain down from all sides. It seems to go on for ever.

In early modern Spain, so the historian Casey says, the cult of the dead occupied and absorbed much of the energy and the resources of the family and the community. Viva la muerte! Unhappy those countries in which men do not continually think of death and in which the guiding principle of life is not the thought that we shall all one day have to lose it, says Unamino.

Helping one's relatives and neighbours to die well was a serious obligation. Friends and relatives would arrive to assist the dying person in reciting prayers. In death as in life, Spaniards of Juan's time thought of prayer as a communal responsibility. ('From Madrid to Purgatory', Eire). It was an opportunity to participate in the greatest moment of man's experience. For although in all countries death is the end, it arrives and the curtain falls, not so in Spain, says Lorca. On the contrary, the curtain only rises at that moment. So like a bullfighter, the Spaniard, focussing on death, chooses to stare down life's most vexing quandary.

For me it is still summer and Juan does not die here until winter comes, so I pay a first exploratory visit to the descalzo Carmelite monastery that provides the stage for his death. The little convento of San Miguel has become the Museo Conventual de San Juan. Monastery and chapel have been considerably enlarged. Scarcely anything of the original structure is visible, but props for the drama are on display.

I sit in what was the simple chapel, the place of Juan's funeral. Now it is a flamboyant baroque Basílica. The nice man in charge of entry to the museum comes in and sits there too. At least his brown habit of the descalzo Carmelite has not been embellished since Juan wore it. Nor has the clangour of the bells of nearby San Pablo, reverberating around me and upstairs in Juan's cell.

On a second visit I penetrate further into the shrine. The desk he used when he visited the nuns in Beas has been brought here. His signature can be made out on a document, Fr Ju de la X. There is a mock-up of the way his cell was when he lay down in it to die, quite small and cramped. There is the very table, plain and utilitarian, on which his body was laid out when lifted from his bed after his death at midnight. I touch the table top fetishistically. In a small glass case I see the tips of the index and middle finger of his right hand, and a tiny iron clasp from the belt he was wearing.

Finally I visit the death cell itself. They have expanded it and painted it and gilded it, and they have given it a great arched and decorated ceiling. They have opened up a side wall of it to look down into the Basílica.

In a precious casket of silver and glass are exposed for veneration the most important relics of the saint which now remain in Úbeda. What I see here are some of Juan's own bones, one tiny arm and one tiny leg.

These old bones set out from La Peñuala to head this way on a very hot day, 28 September 1591. Juan assured his friends that he was going to Úbeda to be cured of some little feverishness, curar de unas calenturillas.

Juan rode on a mule, to rest his inflamed right ankle. He was accompanied by the youth who had delivered the mule to him. Down they came along our familiar road through Vilches, past Arquillos and eventually, after six and a half leagues, six and a half hours travelling at my speed, to the banks of the Guadalimar. No 100 metre steel bridge for them, but the good old stone one. It had five Roman arches. In normal times, as it was, the river flowed only through the central arch, in spate through all five. Here they rested. They sat down in the shade on dry ground under one of the side arches.

Juan had not been eating since the fever came upon him. He had no appetite. The youth offered him food on the way, but he refused. Several times he rejected it. Finally, sitting under the bridge, he said that he would eat, 'some asparagus, if there were any'. A moment later the youth saw, very near, on a flat stone in the river, a bunch of the kind of asparagus that grows among wheat – 'bread asparagus' they called it. The youth fetched it off the stone and, at Juan's insistence, first looked around for the owner of the land and then, not having seen him, left four maravedis on the stone as payment.

Some three, up-hill, hours later they came through the walls into Úbeda by the beautiful, horseshoe-arched gate, The Puerta del Losal. For Juan it was the very end of summer and the evening of his life. I am through this same gate at an earlier season.

To come to the convento of San Miguel we have to stay close to the eastern wall of the city, heading south along narrow streets, 50 metres straight on and then a left turn and just 100 metres to the door of the monastery, a poor and small place, recently opened then.

Juan is welcomed with joy by some of the friars. His former subjects in El Calvario and Granada, they love and admire him and are delighted to hear from the youth of the latest 'miracle' of the asparagus. The prior, on the other hand, receives him coldly. This man of learning is a noted preacher but is sour in his personal relationships. His method is 'to bring others to perfection by the rod'. He tests particularly harshly those who are looked upon by others as saintly. On top of this, he bears a grudge against Juan who, when Vicar-Provincial of Andalusia, had to call him to order once for lack of charity.

The prior decides to lodge Juan in the poorest and narrowest cell, a choice for which he feels profoundly grateful. The prior instructs Juan to be present at all community offices, whatever his state of health.

Within a few days, however, Juan becomes so diseased that he fails to appear in the refectory. The prior sends for him and reprimands him fiercely before all the friars. Juan can only drag himself back to his cell and lie down on his wretched bed-board, never to get up again.

What began as a pimple in the instep of his right foot has become a virulent inflammation that has spread across his foot and ankle and has broken out into five sores. These five wounds mark out the shape of a cross. The largest of them, in the centre, is in the exact place where the nail through Christ's foot is always shown to be. Juan looks upon them with resignation, even with affection, as a constant reminder of his Redeemer. He is suffering from St Anthony's Fire.

A doctor is called. With his scissors he scrapes the infected flesh from the heel and up along the shin bone for two inches of more. He probes among the nerves, cauterises the wounds and sews the skin across them

197

with gut, allowing the bone to remain exposed. Meanwhile Juan lies back, his hands joined on his breast. 'What has your honour done?' he asks the doctor. 'I have opened your reverence's foot and leg'. 'If it is necessary to cut more, well and good, and may the will of our Lord Jesus Christ be done'.

During the operation, and after it, pus flows abundantly. Whole cups are filled with it. Those crowding into the cell are surprised that it does not smell unpleasant. The odour is like musk. One brother even puts it to his lips. The bandages, which are constantly saturated with it and replaced, have the same fragrance. A neighbouring lady and her two daughters are happy to wash them. Even when steeped in pus, and with shreds of flesh clinging to them, they seem to them as pleasant as rose petals. The girls squabble over whose turn it is to do the washing. Women cannot visit Juan, of course, inside the monastery enclosure, but they send him messages of encouragement with the clean linen. Three years later the elder daughter will take the Carmelite habit as a descalza.

The doctor talks around town about his remarkable patient and keeps some of the sweet-scented bandages he peels from Juan's leg. He even tries applying them to other people's wounds. More and more people come to the monastery wanting to help. Another neighbouring lady takes responsibility for preparing his food and sending it to him in a basket. A fourteen-year-old servant girl is allowed, as a child, to bring it into his cell. The supplies become so lavish that he has to ask the benefactress to stop. He cannot thank her enough but he must confine himself to the basic monastic diet.

Many people from the town visit Juan in his cell, watch his doctor at work on his leg, carry off his bandages to keep or to cure sick friends with, and send in gifts of delicacies which he of course dispenses to others. When his narrow cell can hold no more well-wishers, others crowd outside. Musicians are sent for and tune up in the corridor. Juan calls out, 'I am very grateful for the charity you want to show me but it would not be right, when God wants to favour me with these great sufferings I am undergoing, that I should try to soften and moderate them with music and entertainment...The good work these gentlemen want to do in my regard I consider as already done ... give them something and send them away'.

Day by day the physical torment worsens. Ulceration spreads from his leg to his back. A great tumour grows there, as big as a fist, and then opens as a weeping wound. His fever rises. There comes a day when Juan can no longer move himself to change his posture. So they hang from the ceiling a rope. By clinging to this he can shift himself a little. Now he scarcely speaks, but he is thinking. His advice to others has been that it is wise to know how to keep quiet and suffer rather than to pre-occupy oneself with the hereafter. What lies beyond must be a mystery. But he is longing. We long for the final web that separates us from God to be broken, he wrote. And he is burning in his narrow death bed.

> Oh flame of love alive,
> How tenderly you fret
> My soul in its profoundest centre!
> Since now not fugitive,
> Complete now will you yet,
> Break through the veil to sweet encounter.
>
> Oh softly to be burned!
> Oh wound so welcome made!
> Oh gentle hand! His delicate strokes,
> Who eternal life has learned,
> And who all the debts has paid!
> And in killing, death to life revokes.
>
> Oh flaming lamps of fire,
> In brightness of whose splendour
> The very deepest caves of feeling,
> Which were so blind and obscure,
> Now with the strangest wonder
> Heat and light give, in congress with their darling!
>
> As soother and as lover
> You muse within my breast,
> Where you alone live secretly:
> And to breathe you in to savour
> To the full gives glory best
> As delicately you enamour me!

The prior of the little monastery where Juan lay is vexed by it all. He resents the demands upon his budget and he resents the intensity of the focus on the death cell, the crowds, the interest, the sympathy, the talk all around town. He lets his aversion to Juan show. He visits him with cruel remarks and he constrains the freedom of his friars to spend time in the cell. He even hinders the laundering of bandages. When this upsets the friars, Juan always finds an excuse for the prior. And others, from within the monastery, from the wider descalzo Carmelite Order and from the townspeople of Úbeda, visit Juan with love.

Juan sees the language of God in the love these people bring him. The language of God, he writes, is the silent language of love. The word God hears best is just the silence of love. And union of the soul with God is attained when the likeness between the two, that comes from love, is produced, so that two wills are conformed together in one. In the evening of our life, Juan says, the question that is asked of us is love.

After December 6th Juan frequently asks what day it is. On December 7th he is told that he is coming to his end. He says, with a joyful face, that he is making his peace with God. On December 11th he asks for, and receives with great fervour, the viaticum, the preparation for a journey, the Eucharist given to those in danger of death.

It is December 13th and Juan knows that he is dying moment by moment. He wants the prior to come to his cell, where they are reconciled. Juan asks pardon for the trouble and expense he has caused in his illness. The prior asks, in his turn to be forgiven for not having looked after him better. 'Father-prior', Juan replies, 'I am happy and have more than I deserve'. The prior is deeply moved and leaves the cell in tears. He comes back, kneels beside the bed, and asks Juan if he may have his breviary to keep in memory of him. 'I have nothing of my own to give your reverence, all is yours, for you are my Superior,' says Juan.

In the evening Juan receives extreme unction, takes a crucifix in his hands and kisses the feet of it repeatedly. He apologises for not answering questions when he is consumed with pain.

From ten o'clock at night he constantly asks what time it is. Then he asks the friars to go away and rest, for he will call them when it is time. He prays in silence. At half-past eleven his face lights up with joy and he exclaims, 'Now the hour is approaching; call the fathers'. Fourteen or fifteen friars and townsmen crowd into the cell with their lamps. They recite psalms with him, alternately verse by verse, De Profundis and Miserere. Then he receives the Sacred Host. 'Lord, I shall never again see you with mortal eyes,' he exclaims. And, 'What time is it?' They tell him it is not yet twelve. 'At that time I shall be saying matins in the presence of God our Lord'. He asks them to read to him from the Song of Songs. 'What precious pearls,' he sighs.

Shortly before midnight Juan asks them all to leave him, 'For it is time to close the monastery; tonight I have to go and say matins in heaven.' Only one friar remains. Midnight strikes. The bell rings for matins. 'What are they ringing for?' When told it is for matins he exclaims, 'Glory be to God for I shall say them in heaven'. He puts his lips to the crucifix he is holding. He says slowly, 'In manus tuas, Domine, commendo spiritum meum'. He breathes no more.

His lesson to us, the lesson of mysticism, has been, 'We can, while understanding little, love much'.

Here ends Juan's Spanish camino, a path illuminated, thank God, by the pure spark of the sublime. And here ends my Spanish camino too, a path illuminated, thank God, by the odd spark of the ridiculous.

# ON EARTH AS IT IS IN SPAIN – BIBLIOGRAPHY

San Juan de la Cruz. 'Poesías'. Editorial Mirian, Sevilla, 2006

San Juan de la Cruz. 'Escritos Breves'. Editorial de Espiritualidad, Madrid 1983

Saint Jean de la Croix. 'Une Pensée par Jour'. (ed. Mahieu, le père P.), Mediaspaul, 2009.

John of the Cross. 'Ascent of Mount Carmel'. (ed. Carrigan, H.), Paraclete Press, Massachusetts, 2002.

St John of the Cross. 'The Mystical Doctrine' (ed Steuart, R.), Burns & Oates, London, 2002.

St John of the Cross. 'The Living Flame of Love', (trans. Obbard, E.) N Y City, 2004.

Campbell, R. 'St John of the Cross – The Poems'. The Harville Press, London, 2000.

Jones, K. 'The Poems of St John of the Cross'. Burns & Oates. London 1993

Brenan, G. 'St John of the Cross, His Life and Poetry'. Cambridge University Press 1973.

Crisógono de Jesus. 'The Life of St John of the Cross'. (trans. Pond, K) Longmans, London 1958

Sesé, B. 'Petite Vie de St Jean de la Croix'. Desclée de Brouwer. 2003.

---

Baigent, M. 'The Inquisition'. Penguin Books, 2000.

Barea, A. 'The Clash'. Faber & Faber Ltd, 1945.

Barrès, M. 'Greco ou le Secret de Tolede'. Émile-Paul Éditeurs, 1912

Beevor, A. 'The Spanish Civil War'. Cassell, 1999

Bennassar, B. 'L'Histoire des Espagnols'. Armand Collin 1985.

Bennasar, B. 'L'Homme Espagnol'. Hachette. 1975.

Bilinkoff, J. 'The Ávila of St Teresa'. Cornell University Press, 1989.

Brenan, G. 'The Face of Spain'. Penguin, 1987.

Brenan G. 'South from Granada'. Penguin, 1963.

du Boulay, S. 'Teresa of Ávila'. Hodder and Stoughton, 1991.

Boyd, A. 'The Companion Guide to Madrid and Central Spain'. Companion Guides, 2002.

Byron, W. 'Cervantes a Biography'. Cassell, 1979.

Cañada, P. 'Baeza en San Juan de la Cruz'. Artes, Gráficas Publimax, 1998.

Casey, J. 'Early Modern Spain'. Routledge, 1999.

Cervantes, M. 'The Life and Achievements of Don Quixote de la Mancha', (trans. Motteux). George Newnes, 1902.

Christian, W. 'Local Religion in Sixteenth Century Spain'. Princeton, 1981.

Crastre, V. 'Toledo', (trans. Peppard, N). George G Harrap and Co Ltd, 1957.

Cugno, A. 'St John of the Cross,' (trans. Wall, B). Burns & Oates, 1982.

Dombrowski, D. 'St John of the Cross. An Appreciation'. State University of New York Press, 1992.

Dostoievsky, F. 'The Brothers Karamazov'. (trans. Magarshack). Penguin Books, 1958.

Eire, C. 'From Madrid to Purgatory'. Cambridge University Press, 1995.

Elliott, J. 'Imperial Spain 1469-1716'. Penguin Books, 2002.

Erlanger, P. 'Isabelle la Catholique'. Perrin, 1996.

D'Espagnet, B. 'On Physics and Philosophy'. Princeton University Press, 2006.

Ford, R. 'Gatherings from Spain'. Everyman's Library, 1970.

Giono, J. 'Colline'. Grasset, 1929.

Gorer, G. 'Africa Dances'. Eland, London, 2003.

Green, T. 'Inquisition – the Reign of Fear'. Macmillan, 2007.

Hamilton, A. 'Heresy and Mysticism in Sixteenth Century Spain'. James Clarke and Co., 1992.

Homza, L. 'Religious Authority in the Spanish Renaissance'. The John Hopkins University Press, 2000.

Hume, M. 'The Spanish People'. William Heinemann, 1901.

Irwin, R. 'The Alhambra'. Profile Books, 2005.

Jotiscky, A. 'The Carmelites and Antiquity'. OUP, 2002.

Kagan, R. 'Students and Society in Early Modern Spain'. The John Hopkins University Press., 1974.

Kamen, H. 'The Disinherited'. Penguin Books, 2008.

Kamen H. 'Inquisition and Society in Spain'. Weidenfeld and Nicholson, 1985.

Kamen, H. 'Spain 1469-1714. A Society of Conflict'. Longman, 1983.

Kealy, T. 'Bacon's Shadow'. Prospect Magazine, October 2005.

Lalaguna, J. 'A Travellers History of Spain'. Phoenix, 2002.

Lauzeral, P. 'Quand l'Amour Tisse un Destin'. Mediaspaul, 1985.

Lorca, F. 'Jeu et Théorie de Duende', (trans. Amselem, L) Editions Allia, 2008.

Lorca, F. 'Selected Poems'. Penguin Classics, 2001.

Lynch, J. 'Spain 1516-1598'. Blackwell, 1991.

Machado, A. 'Campos de Castilla'. Ediciones Cátedra, 2006.

Machado, A. 'The Landscape of Castille', (trans. Berg, M) White Pine Press, Buffalo, NY, 2005.

Machado, A. 'Poesía'. Alianza Editorial, 2008.

Martz, L. 'Poverty and Welfare in Habsburg Spain'. Cambridge University Press, 1983.

Mc Greal, W. 'John of the Cross'. Triumph, Liguori, Missouri, 1996.

Menéndez Pidal, R. 'The Spaniards in their History', (trans Starkie, W). London, 1950

Montalva, P. 'Beas y santa Teresa'. Editorial de Espiritualidad, 1975.

Morton, H. 'A Stranger in Spain'. Methuen and Co Ltd., 2006.

Ortega y Gasset, J. 'Invertebrate Spain'. George Allen and Unwin Ltd., 1937.

Ortega y Gasset, J. 'Meditations on Quixote', (trans. Rugg, E) W W Norton and Coy Inc NY, 1961.

Peers, E. 'The Complete Works of St Teresa of Jesus', Vol III. London, Sheed and Ward, 1946.

Peers, E. 'Handbook to the Life and Times of St Teresa and St John of the Cross'. Burns & Oates, London, 1954.

Peers, E. 'St Teresa of Jesus'. Faber and Faber, 1953.

Peers, E. 'Spanish Mysticism'. Methuen and Co Ltd., 1924.

Perez J. L'Espagne du XVleme Siècle.' Armand Collin, 2004.

Petrie, Sir C. 'Philip II of Spain'. Eyre and Spottiswoode, 1963.

Pritchett, V. 'Marching Spain' Ernest Benn Ltd. London, 1928.

Pritchett, V. 'The Spanish Temper'. Chatto and Windus, London, 1954.

Rawlings, H. 'Church, Religion and Society in Early Modern Spain.' Palgrave, 2002.

Ruiz, T. 'Spanish Society 1400-1600'. Pearson Education Ltd, 2001.

Sagne, J. 'Lire et Relire saint Jean de la Croix'. Editions du Carmel, Toulouse, 2008.

Stinissen, G. 'Découvre-moi Ta Présence'. Les Editions du Cerf, Paris, 2008.

Trend, J. 'The Language and History of Spain'. Hutchinson's University Library, London, 1953.

Unamuno, M.de. 'Essays and Soliloquies,' (trans. Crawford Flitch, J). George G. Harrap and Co Ltd., 1925.